SUDOKU
CROSSWORDS   WORD SEARCHES
LOGIC PUZZLES & SURPRISES!

mind
STRETCHERS

VOLUME 10

EDITED BY ALLEN D. BRAGDON

Reader's
Digest

Copyright © 2020 by Trusted Media Brands, Inc.

ISBN 978-1-62145-471-7

Address any comments about Mind Stretchers Volume 10 to:
Reader's Digest Adult Trade Books
44 South Broadway
White Plains, NY 10601

Visit us on the Web in the United States at rd.com
and in Canada at readersdigest.ca

Printed in China

10 9 8 7 6 5 4 3 2

Contents

Dear Puzzler,

Here I am—figuratively chewing my pencil as I try to concentrate.

The puzzles in this edition of *Mind Stretchers* demand concentration while challenging a variety of brain skills, including our ability to remember.

Most complaints about memory have nothing to do with the actual ability of the brain to remember things. They come from a failure to focus properly on the task at hand. The brain tunes out inputs that don't spell S-U-R-V-I-V-A-L. Remembering the name of your girlfriend's cat, for example, is probably not the most important thing on your mind, and if you are to succeed you need to stop for a moment and concentrate on linking its name to someone or something that will help you to recall it in the future.

As the brain ages, vocabulary may remain strong in the memory, but the ability to spot meanings and search for the word you are looking for slows down:

Two elderly couples were visiting each other and went out for a walk. The two men, John and Joe, were walking ahead.

'We found a great restaurant last night', said Joe.

'What is it called?' John asked.

They stopped for a moment. Joe scratched his head and then said, 'You know, we've been married for over fifty years, but my memory's not so great. Help me out. What is the name of the flower that has a really thorny stem? The red one that is popular on Valentine's Day?'

John replied, 'You mean the rose?'

Joe said, 'Yes that's it, of course—the rose!'

He turned back and called out to his wife, 'Rose, what was the name of that restaurant we were in last night?'

Language puzzles exercise those circuits that can help lessen forgetful moments and shorten their duration, but memory cannot become learning without concentration, and without regular maintenance, concentration shrinks with age. Puzzles in this edition of *Mind Stretchers* provide many opportunities for improving and strengthening this important ability and many other useful brain skills:

- pattern and pathfinding puzzles will strengthen your powers of concentration in the same way that physical exercises build aerobic stamina;
- logic and memory puzzles will put a strain on your working memory because you must keep some variables in mind while you test them against others—this frontal-lobe skill is crucial to productive thinking and requires fierce concentration;
- visual and mechanical puzzles will stretch your visual-spatial mental muscles for use in design, architecture, mechanical engineering, exploration and construction;
- divergent thinking puzzles will encourage your ability to think 'outside the box' and see links where others see standard differences—an ability that pays off in any profession;
- puzzles involving calculation are important to try—even if you are not a numbers person—for they light up many different parts of the brain at once.

Now, what was that cat called? Large spring?

Ah, that's it—Maxwell!

Allen D. Bragdon

Mind Stretchers Puzzle Editor

Meet the Authors

Allen D. Bragdon

Allen is a member of the Society for Neuroscience, founding editor of *Games* magazine and editor of the Playspace daily puzzle column, formerly syndicated internationally by *The New York Times*. The author of dozens of books of professional and academic examinations and how-to instructions in practical skills, Allen is also the director of the Brainwaves Center.

PeterFrank

Founded in 2000, PeterFrank is a dynamic, full-service content provider specialising in media content. They have more than twenty years of experience in publishing management, art/design and software development for newspapers, consumer magazines, special interest publications and new media.

John M. Samson

John M. Samson is currently editor of Simon & Schuster's *Mega Crossword Series*. His crosswords have appeared on cereal boxes, rock album covers, quilts, jigsaw puzzles, posters, advertisements, newspapers, magazines and sides of buildings. John also enjoys painting and writing for the stage and screen.

Sam Bellotto Jr.

Sam Bellotto Jr. has been making puzzles professionally since 1979. He has been a regular contributor to Simon & Schuster, *The New York Times*, Random House, and magazines such as *Back Stage*, *Central New*

York, *Public Citizen* and *Music Alive!* Bellotto's Rochester, New York-based company, Crossdown, develops word-puzzle computer games and crossword construction software.

BrainSnack®

The internationally registered trademark BrainSnack® stands for challenging, language-independent, logical puzzles and mind games for kids, young adults and adults. Whether they are made by hand, such as visual puzzles, or generated by a computer, such as sudoku, all puzzles are tested by the target group they were made for before they are made available.

Auspac Media is the oldest privately owned syndication company in Australia and supplies content to newspapers, magazines, educational departments, textbooks, websites and tablet applications. They represent numerous Australian creators and various international agencies. Their array of material covers word puzzles, number puzzles, quizzes, crosswords, horoscopes, comics and magazine articles.

Christine Lovatt, founder of Lovatts Publishing Group, has been creating crosswords and puzzles for more than 30 years. She started creating crosswords at age 12 as a hobby, and her crosswords now appear in major magazines and newspapers around the world, and more recently websites. She also publishes more than twenty puzzle magazine titles as well as launching the online game site YouPlay.com.

Meet the Puzzles

Mind Stretchers is filled with a delightful mix of classic and new puzzle types. To help you get started, here are instructions, tips and examples for each.

WORD GAMES

Crossword Puzzles

Clues. Clues. Clues.

Clues are the deciding factor that determines crossword-solving difficulty. Many solvers mistakenly think strange and unusual words are what make a puzzle challenging. In reality, crossword constructors generally try to avoid grid esoterica, opting for familiar words and expressions.

For example, here are some actual clues you'll be encountering and their respective difficulty levels:

LEVEL 1   Capital of Iran
LEVEL 2   Unbleached linen
LEVEL 3   Bolus
LEVEL 4   *Alfred* composer

Clues to amuse. Clues to educate. Clues to challenge your mind.

All the clues are there—what's needed now is your answers.

Happy solving!

Word Searches

by PeterFrank

Both kids and grownups love 'em, making word searches one of the most popular types of puzzle. In a word search, the challenge is to find hidden words within a grid of letters. In the typical puzzle, words can be found in vertical columns, horizontal rows or along diagonals, with the letters of the words running either forward or backward. Usually, you'll be given a list of words to find. But to make word searches harder, puzzle writers sometimes just point you in the right direction—they might tell you to find 25 foods, for example. Other twists include allowing words to take right turns, or leaving letters out of the grid.

Hints: *One of the most reliable and efficient searching methods is to scan each row from top to bottom for the first letter of the word. So if you are looking for 'violin', you would look for the letter 'v'. When you find one, look at all the letters that surround it for the second letter of the word (in this case, 'i'). Each time you find a correct two-letter combination (in this case, 'vi'), you can then scan either for the correct three-letter combination ('vio') or the whole word.*

Word Sudoku

by PeterFrank

Sudoku puzzles have become hugely popular, and our word sudoku puzzles bring the much-loved challenge to word puzzlers.

The basic sudoku puzzle is a 9 x 9 square grid, split into 9 square regions, each containing 9 cells. You need to complete the grid so that each row, each column and each 3 x 3 frame contains the nine letters from the black box above the grid.

There is always a hidden nine-letter word in the diagonal from top left to bottom right.

EXAMPLE   SOLUTION

NUMBER GAMES

Sudoku

by PeterFrank

The original sudoku number format is amazingly popular the world over due to its simplicity and challenge.

The basic sudoku puzzle is a 9 x 9 square grid, split into 9 square regions, each containing 9 cells. Complete the grid so that each row, each column and each 3 x 3 frame contains every number from 1 to 9.

EXAMPLE   SOLUTION

As well as classic sudoku puzzles, you'll also find sudoku X puzzles, where the main diagonals must also include every number from 1 to 9, and sudoku twins with two overlapping grids.

Kakuro

by PeterFrank

These puzzles are like crosswords with numbers. There are clues across and down, but the clues are numbers. The solution is a sum which adds up to the clue number.

Each number in a black area is the sum of the numbers that you have to enter in the next empty boxes. The empty boxes that make up the sum are called a run. The sum of the across run is written above the diagonal in the black area, while the sum of the down run is written below the diagonal.

Runs can contain only the numbers 1 through to 9, and each number in a run can only be used once. The grey boxes contain only odd numbers and the white contain only even numbers.

EXAMPLE   SOLUTION

LOGIC PUZZLES

Binairo

by PeterFrank

Binairo puzzles look similar to sudoku puzzles. They are just as simple and challenging but that is where the similarity ends.

There are two versions: odd and even. The even puzzles feature a 12 x 12 grid. You need to complete the grid with zeros and ones, until there are 6 zeros and 6 ones in every row and every column. No more than two of the same number can be next to or under each other. Rows or columns with exactly the same combination are not allowed.

EXAMPLE   SOLUTION

The odd puzzles feature an 11 x 11 grid. You need to complete the grid with zeros and ones until there are 5 zeros and 6 ones in every row and column.

Keep Going

In this puzzle, start on a blank square of your choice and connect as many blank squares as possible with one single continuous line.

You can only connect squares along vertical and horizontal lines, not along diagonals. You must continue the connecting line up until the next obstacle—i.e. the rim of the box, a black square or a square that has already been used.

You can change direction at any obstacle you meet. Each square can only be used once. The number of blank squares left unused is marked in the upper square. There is more than one solution, but we only include one solution in our answer key.

EXAMPLE   SOLUTION

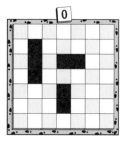 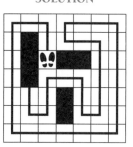

Number Cluster

by PeterFrank

Number Cluster puzzles are language-free, logical numerical problems. They consist of cubes on a 6 x 6 grid. Numbers have been placed in some of the cubes, while the rest are empty. Your challenge is to complete the grid by creating runs of the same number and length as the number supplied. So where a cube with the number 5 has been included on the grid, you need to create a run of five number 5s, including the cube already shown. The run can be horizontal, vertical, or both horizontal and vertical.

EXAMPLE   SOLUTION

Word Pyramid

Each word in the pyramid has the letters of the word above it, plus a new letter.

Start with the answer to No.1 and work your way to the base of the pyramid to complete the word pyramid.

Sport Maze

This puzzle is presented on a 6 x 6 grid. Your starting point is indicated by a red cell with a ball and a number. Your objective is to draw the shortest route from the ball to the goal, the only square without a number. You can only move along vertical and horizontal lines, but not along diagonals. The figure on each square indicates the number of squares the ball must be moved in the same direction. You can change direction at each stop.

EXAMPLE　　　　SOLUTION

Cage the Animals

This puzzle presents you with a zoo divided into a 16 x 16 grid. The different animals on the grid need to be separated. Draw lines that will completely divide up the grid into smaller squares, with exactly one animal per square. The squares should not overlap.

EXAMPLE　　　　　SOLUTION

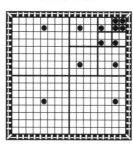

Throughout *Mind Stretchers* you will find unique mazes, visual conundrums and other colourful challenges. Each comes with a new name and unique instructions. Our best advice? Patience and perseverance. Your eyes will need time to unravel the visual secrets.

BrainSnack® Puzzles

To solve a BrainSnack® puzzle, you must think logically. You'll need to use one or several strategies to detect direction, differences and/or similarities, associations, calculations, order, spatial insight, colours, quantities and distances. A BrainSnack® ensures that all the brain's capacities are fully engaged. These are brain sports at their best!

Weather Charts

We all want to know the weather forecast, and here's your chance to figure it out! Arrows are scattered on a grid. Each arrow points in the direction of a space where a weather symbol should be, but the symbols cannot touch each other vertically, horizontally or diagonally. A symbol cannot be placed on top of an arrow. Determine where the symbols should be placed.

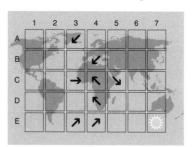

BRAIN TEASERS

You'll also find more than 100 short brain teasers scattered throughout these pages. These puzzles, found on the bottom of the page, will give you a little light relief from the more intense puzzles while still challenging you. Some of the more difficult puzzles have an example of how to solve the puzzle on its first occurrence (the page number is noted below).

But wait—there's more!

There are additional brain teasers at the top of odd numbered pages, organised into two categories:

• **QUICK!:** These tests challenge your ability to instantly calculate numbers or recall well-known facts.

• **DO YOU KNOW…:** These more demanding questions probe the depth of your knowledge of facts and trivia.

ANSWERS!

Answers to all the puzzles are found beginning on page 175, and are organised by the page number on which the puzzle appears.

For the answers to the **Quick!** and the **Do You Know** … brain teasers, go to www.mindstretchers.com.au/answers or www.mindstretchers.co.nz/answers

Master Class: Get in the Mood to Think

David Gamon is a longtime friend and co-author. He has his doctorate in linguistics and his mind in constant motion. We asked him how he gets in a mood to think hard. We have edited his response for space.

Our culture tends to draw distinctions between 'work' and 'play' that the brain does not make. The following list is inspired by the insight that it's good for your brain to play—not just as a break from work, but in order to put the brain into the mood to work.

1. Get a dopamine high

Dopamine is a neurotransmitter, a natural chemical released by the brain to carry signals from one electrically charged cell to other cells. As the cells start to work, dopamine changes the person's conscious mood to a calm, alert sense that 'all is right with the world'.

The dopamine networks evolved to encourage the human brain to engage in these specialised survival functions:

1. to explore new things in terms of past experience;
2. to solve problems in creative ways;
3. to practice and maintain the kinds of cognitive flexibility and mental focus needed for abstract reasoning, logic and many of the left-brain skills used in scientific thinking.

Dopamine rewards you for doing mental work, especially when the tasks are novel and interesting.

Warm Up Your Dopamine Systems

In the puzzles below, what goes in the blank space to continue the sequence? Each puzzle has a different logic to the pattern you have to figure out to get the answer. As you keep looking for a new strategy, the ongoing novelty helps to keep your dopamine levels high. The puzzles start out easy and then get gradually harder, but the harder the problem, the better it feels to solve it.

Blowhard hardhat hatcheck ___mate

Snit in snot on prod or mode __

Gum gun bar bat lip ____

Bird crane stretch sprint run snag lozenge mint ____ beak

7913 992 488 569 72155 614 ___

37210 2 19903 1 48737 3 52209 9 47391 ___

(The answers are at the end of this Master Class.)

2. Stop me if you've heard this one ...

Humour is an act of cognitive restructuring that goes well beyond the physical act of laughing. It creates a mental and emotional distance from a potentially stressful situation or problem. It also may change perspective enough to lead to a better solution to the problem. The kind of set-shifting and cognitive flexibility leading up to the emotional sensation of humour also invites creativity. It is a form of mental exercise that's a form of cognitive play. It oils the cogs of cogitation.

Maybe the sensation of humour is part of an acknowledgment that not all contradictions need to be resolved. Here's a favourite example, a joke attributed to the Danish nuclear physicist Niels Bohr in Werner Heisenberg's *Science and Religion*: 'One of our neighbours in Tisvilde once fixed a horseshoe over the door to his house. When a common friend asked him, "But are you really superstitious? Do you honestly believe that this horseshoe will bring you luck?" he replied, "Of course not; but they say it works even if you don't believe in it."'

The humour seems to lie in the innocent truth within a logical contradiction—the professed, sober disbelief in the good luck power of the horseshoe alongside the impulse to hedge bets.

Here's another Bohrism to tickle logical thinking: 'Never express yourself more clearly than you can think.'

3. Go around in circles

'Convergent thinking' is supposed to lead to a single right answer. (IQ tests tend to have questions with a single right answer, whether you agree with it or not.)

To limber up the rigorously logical side of your brain, try playing with puzzles such as the one below. To get the answer, you have to follow the consequences of each statement, keep them clearly in mind, and keep going until one doesn't lead to a contradiction.

A Logic Puzzle

Here are five statements. All may be true, or only some, or only one, or none at all:

1. Only one of these statements is false.
2. Only two of these statements are false.
3. Only three of these statements are false.
4. Only four of these statements are false.
5. All five of these statements are false.

Which, if any, of the five statements is true? (The answer is at the end of this Master Class.)

4. Listen to all of your brains

There are many brains inside the human cranium, each one with its unique way of processing information. Many of them go about their work inside completely subconscious systems. They are where most 'hunches', 'gut feelings', 'intuitions' and, incidentally, 'dreams', come from.

When the conscious mind is working on a conceptually challenging problem, those other parts of the brain may be at work while the thinking mind's back is turned.

To benefit from their insights, admit they are there and learn to listen to their subtle voices.

When he was an undergraduate at MIT, Richard Feynman taught himself to remain consciously aware, in sleep, of the content of his dreams and, in some ways, to control them. It sounds bizarre, but it's not hard to learn. In a lucid dream state, try feeding your dreaming mind whatever puzzles you want to give it. It is likely to come up with an unconventional representation of a solution.

5. Watch the stress

Creativity thrives better in a 'rest and digest' brain state than in a 'fight or flight' one. In fact, stomach-churning anxiety and healthy curiosity are so incompatible that it's virtually impossible to feel both at once. Acute stress switches off the brain networks used for complex thought, abstract problem solving and knowledge retrieval.

6. Ponder paradoxes

The point of pondering a Zen Buddhist koan ('What is the sound of one hand clapping?' is a classic example) is to transcend the limits of the rational mind. Paradoxes invite different ways of looking at things. That's the first step to the kind of original thinking that nudges the mind into entertaining questions other people haven't even thought of.

Here are a few examples:

There's no such thing as nonexistence.
I am not really me.
'No' and 'meaning' have no meaning.

7. Be willing to believe that what you've been taught might be wrong

When Descartes left his formal studies to devote himself to figuring things out for himself, he eventually decided that there were only two things he knew for sure. The one he's most famous for was that he existed. (The other one was that God existed.) Once he had demolished all the time-honoured structures, the building he erected was decidedly different from the one he had demolished.

8. Just do the opposite

Many interesting insights come from turning problems on their head. Here is an example from linguistics:

The real patterns of mental grammar are to be discovered not in the 'correct' things people say but in the errors they inadvertently make. The errors reveal the patterns that are least likely to be of the artificial, prescriptive sort they were taught in school.

Freud had the same kind of insight when he chose to study the human psyche by paying attention to slips of the tongue.

The solution may lie in considering why the hound did not bark.

9. Invite accidents

Don't blunt your curiosity by what it is you started out looking for in a bunch of data. Many scientific discoveries are serendipitous—they arise inadvertently from research that was intended to answer a completely different question. As the saying goes: 'Am I really lost, or am I just someplace I've never been before?'

10. Don't make lists before you play

Let your mind roam free to play with your needs. Most people sit down first to make a list of steps to achieve a 'goal'. It may be a good list leading to the wrong goal.

Allen D. Bragdon

ANSWERS!

Warm Up Your Dopamine Systems

1. check (mate)
2. do
3. lit
4. bill
5. 9
6. 9

A Logic Puzzle

The fourth statement: If it's true, then the other four statements are false—no contradiction.

★ For Starters

ACROSS

1 Triumph, succeed
5 Finetunes
9 First milk secreted after birth
10 Daub
11 Sound of a pig
12 Dependent on events or circumstances
14 Death announcement
15 Awkward, graceless
18 Spotted South American feline
19 Richness
22 Able to live on land and in water
24 Abominable snowman
26 Grub
27 Attend a party uninvited
28 Thick glove
29 Unchecked

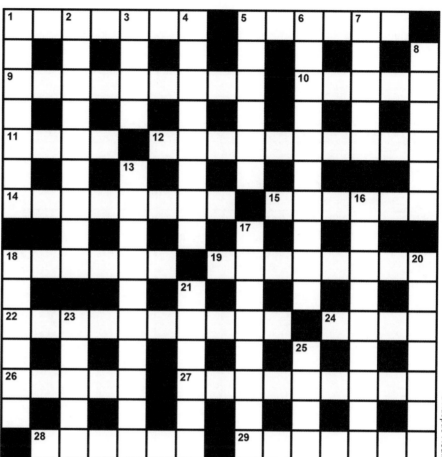

©Auspac Media

DOWN

1 Small flute
2 Sweetbriar
3 Too
4 Port side
5 Salad vegetable
6 Replaceable, inessential
7 Stab
8 Sculpture of a human figure

13 Self-taught individual
16 Barren region of Western Ireland
17 Spit out food when choking or laughing
18 Source of divine revelation
20 Descriptive nickname

21 Language made up of elements of two or more tongues
23 Zoroastrian
25 Layer of impurities on a liquid's surface

★★ Number Cluster

Complete the grid by forming adjoining clusters that consist of as many cubes as the number shown on the cubes. At cube 5, for example, you will have to make a cluster of five adjoining cubes. The number already shown in a cube is counted as part of the cluster. You can only place your cubes along horizontal and/or vertical lines, never diagonally.

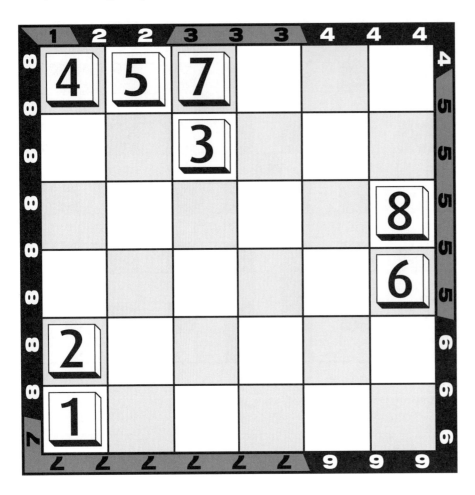

ONE LETTER LESS OR MORE

The word on the right side contains the letters of the word on the left side minus the letter shown in the middle. What is that word? One letter is already in the right place.

★ BrainSnack®—Touchdown

What digit should replace the question mark in the score below?

UNCANNY TURN

Rearrange the letters of the words below to form a new word or phrase that is related to it in some way. The answer can be one or more words. Example: The letters in THEY SEE can be rearranged to spell THE EYES.

ONE LIVE WITNESS

★ Quick and Easy

ACROSS

1 Pierce with a knife
4 Broadcast, strewn
10 Walking unsteadily
11 Meataxe
12 Section of a newspaper article
13 Improvised, impromptu (2-3)
14 Government financial officer
16 Link, bind
17 Coach
18 Examination of a joint by insertion of an instrument
22 Trainee officer
23 Detachment protecting the back of an army
25 Mortification
26 Unimportant, petty
27 Earnest and purposeful undertaking
28 Long protruding tooth

©Auspac Media

DOWN

2 Canaan, to Abraham and his descendants (3,8,4)
3 Carry to a place
4 Giant American cactus
5 Intoxicating drink
6 Dictionary of synonyms
7 Radical supporters of social upheaval
8 Long-lasting
9 Line of latitude 23.5° north or south of the equator
15 Italian restaurant
17 Two-wheeled transport
19 Capital of Ontario
20 Nuclear power generator
21 Sings in the Swiss manner
24 Flash of light

★ United States of America

All the words listed are hidden vertically, horizontally or diagonally—in both directions. The letters that remain unused form a sentence from left to right.

```
O K L A H O M A M O N T A N A
T H E N L A W I S C O N S I N
V A M E A A M E C R G O A I C
I A L K D I B O S G E M R P N
R R M A R Y L A N D R R I O E
G B V N S O A I M A O E Z B W
I E L S R K M N D A Y V O A J
N R D A E O A I N D I A N A E
I H D S Y G R S R O I A A V R
A O E W I O I D C F I R O M S
A D M H L O E I R S I G A E E
O E C F N G X V I E S P R U Y
C I C I I E E U A M E A K H R
M S L C M H O O A N W T A A N
A L D W S L A I R A L W N O R
I A E W H O W A L G A S S B O
N N K R O Y W E N I I R A N I
E D N F L O D R I E N A S C E
```

ALABAMA
ALASKA
ARIZONA
ARKANSAS
COLORADO
DELAWARE
FLORIDA
GEORGIA
HAWAII
ILLINOIS
INDIANA
KANSAS
LOUISIANA
MAINE
MARYLAND
MICHIGAN
MONTANA
NEVADA
NEW JERSEY
NEW MEXICO
NEW YORK
OKLAHOMA
OREGON
RHODE ISLAND
VERMONT
VIRGINIA
WISCONSIN
WYOMING

CHANGE ONE

Change one letter in each of these two words to form a common two-word phrase. Example: HAT DOT. Answer: HOT DOG

TWITCH IN

_____

★★ Keep Going

Starting on a blank square of your choice, connect as many blank squares as possible with one single continuous line. You can only connect squares along vertical and horizontal lines, not along diagonal lines. You must continue the connecting line up until the next obstacle, i.e. the rim of the box, a black square or a square that has already been used. You can change direction at any obstacle you meet. Each square can be used only once. The number of blank squares that will be left unused is marked in the upper square. There is more than one solution. We show only one solution.

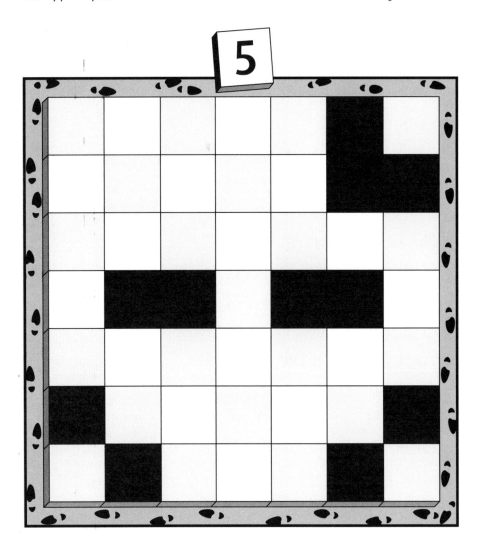

FRIENDS

What same word or affix can be added to the following to make new words?

ANGEL BISHOP DEACON DUCHESS DUKE ENEMY WAY

★ Quick and Easy

ACROSS

1 Study of fossils
9 Lacking any scent
10 Artless, ingenuous
11 Toss
12 Australian state
14 Metrical foot of a long and short syllable
15 Flying an aircraft without engine power
17 Native of Tel Aviv
20 Deer meat
22 Retribution
23 Perfumed powder
25 Sportsground
26 Straightened up again
27 Metal bar with holes for the fingers, used in fighting

DOWN

1 Stipulation, rider
2 Skulk
3 Put to death
4 Savings kept in reserve (4,3)
5 All-knowing
6 Art of paper folding
7 Profit, return
8 Coloured paper thrown at weddings
13 Knot used to shorten a rope
16 Wholesale killing of an ethnic group
18 Verse where the opening words form a repeated refrain
19 Dip into water
20 The former New Hebrides
21 Wrench
22 Practical joke
24 Filth

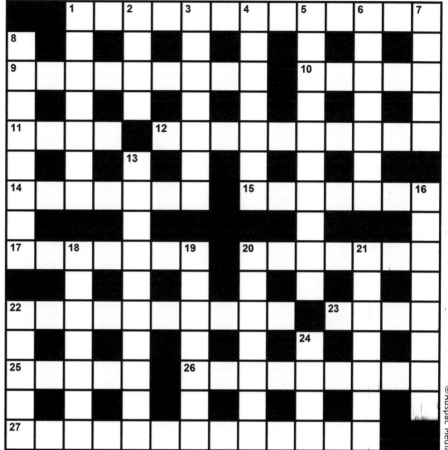

©Auspac Media

★★★ Sudoku

Fill in the grid so that each row, each column and each 3 x 3 frame contains every number from 1 to 9.

			6					
4		2			7			
	7	8	2					
7	8	4					2	
2		6	1				3	5
	5	3						
8	4		7	3	5			
				9			7	4
3				6	2	8		9

DOODLE PUZZLE

A doodle puzzle is a combination of images, letters and/or numbers that represent a word or a concept. If you cannot solve a doodle puzzle, do not look at the answer right away. Think hard—and outside the box.

★★★ Sport Maze

Draw the shortest route from the golf ball to the hole. You can only move along vertical and horizontal lines, not along diagonal lines. The figure in each square indicates the number of squares the ball must be moved in the same direction. You can change directions at each stop. You can also retrace your path. The hole must be entered with the exact number of moves shown on the last square.

	5	4	3	5	2
3	4	3	3	2	5
1	2	2	3	4	4
1	1	2	1	4	3
2	1	4	1	3	1
3	5	5	3	1	1

ONE LETTER LESS OR MORE

The word on the right side contains the letters of the word on the left side minus the letter shown in the middle. What is that word? One letter is already in the right place.

| B | A | C | H | E | L | O | R | -B | | | | L | | | |

★ Quick and Easy

ACROSS

1 Impossible to subdue
9 Sugar pea
10 Drily amusing
11 See eye to eye
12 Venetian oarsman
13 Sirenian mammal of coastal America
14 Vacation
16 Member of a Caucasian minority in Russia
18 Play or film that includes songs
21 Yacht with twin parallel hulls
23 Examination of business accounts
24 Without illumination
25 Roman name for Scotland
27 The art of painting likenesses of people

DOWN

1 Lack of knowledge
2 Most profound
3 Low
4 Pharaoh whose tomb was discovered in 1922

5 Sleeping bag
6 Common intestinal bacteria (1,4)
7 Chemically preserve a dead body
8 Churchmen
12 Seller of fruit and vegetables

15 Moral dissipation
16 Spiny succulent plant
17 Pet rodent
19 Berlin prison that housed Nazi war criminals
20 Deadly
22 Bulbous flower
26 Hawaiian garland

©Auspac Media

★ Word Sudoku

Complete the grid so that each row, each column and each 3 x 3 frame contains the nine letters from the black box below. A nine-letter word is hidden in the diagonal from top left to bottom right.

A E G I M S T U Z

		G						Z
		M		Z				I
						M		E
	E						U	
						S		T
M			S	U	A			
G			U	E	I	T		
	Z					U	E	G
	A	E			T	I	M	

SANDWICH

What five-letter word belongs between the word on the left and the word on the right, so that the first and second word, and the second and third word, each form a common compound word?

O V E R __ __ __ __ __ O V E R

★★ BrainSnack®—Crazy Cube

Which of the blocks numbered from 1 to 9 needs to be removed so that you can combine the three large parts into a single cube?

LETTERBLOCKS

Move the letter blocks around to form two words, one on the top line, the other on the bottom line, that can be associated with chess. Letters can be moved from one line to the other.

A R B T E T Y _ _ _ _ _ _ _
P N O N I E G _ _ _ _ _ _ _

★ Quick and Easy

ACROSS

1 Floating mass of frozen water
5 Surgical knife
10 Official language of Pakistan
11 Most populous American state
12 Jewish Day of Atonement (3,6)
13 Plants used in cookery and medicine
15 Person or thing bringing bad luck
17 Pants
18 Extensive view
20 Spanish-American cattle farm
22 North African nation
23 Surgical ties
26 Number of people present
27 Stink
28 Liquorice flavour
29 One of the Romance languages

© Auspac Media

DOWN

2 Knick-knack
3 Stopped short, jibbed
4 Give-and-take
6 Part of a sleeve
7 Charity, generosity
8 Capital of Scotland
9 Pictures accompanying text
14 Sporting competition
16 Great ape of Borneo and Sumatra (5-4)
19 Subjugate, tyrannise
21 Nonaligned
24 Type of colonic irrigation
25 Rim

★ Binairo

Complete the grid with zeros and ones until there are six zeros (0) and six ones (1) in every row and every column. No more than two of the same number can be next to or under each other. Rows or columns with exactly the same content are not allowed. There is only one valid solution per puzzle.

					I		I				
						I		I			I
O	I		I		I						I
									O		
		O		O	O				O		
		O				I					I
						O					
	O										
		O	O			I	I		I		
						I					O
I				I			O				O
	I		I		O	O			I		

REPOSITION PREPOSITION

Unscramble the words below and find a three-word phrase.

I DID NOTATION

_____ _____ _____

★ Spot the Differences

There are nine differences between these two images. Can you find them? Circle the differences on the image on the right.

DOUBLETALK

What eight-letter word means 'a doorway' or 'delight'?

_ _ _ _ _ _ _ _

★ Quick and Easy

ACROSS

- **1** Bad-tempered, irascible
- **9** Large sea
- **10** Nourishment
- **11** Abrasion
- **12** Ingenuousness
- **13** Out of favour
- **15** Rope fibre
- **16** Musical, songlike
- **18** Event combining swimming, cycling and running
- **21** Held fast
- **22** Paraguayan monetary unit
- **24** Small republic, surrounded by Italy (3,6)
- **26** Excessive, inordinate
- **27** Financier, impresario

DOWN

- **1** Transparent
- **2** Unremitting, interminable
- **3** Completely destroyed
- **4** Set of tools
- **5** Dried grapes
- **6** All-embracing
- **7** Japanese mainland
- **8** Sick
- **12** Residence for the aged or infirm (7,4)
- **14** Temple of Athena on the Acropolis
- **16** Maintain communications with
- **17** Pirate
- **19** Speak badly of
- **20** Sounds
- **23** Snake
- **25** Sprite, gremlin

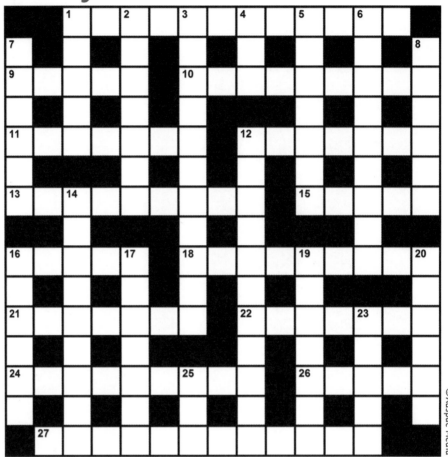

©Auspac Media

★ Cage the Animals

Draw the lines that will completely divide up the grid into smaller squares, representing cages, with exactly one animal per cage. Each cage can be as small as a single grid square. The cages cannot overlap.

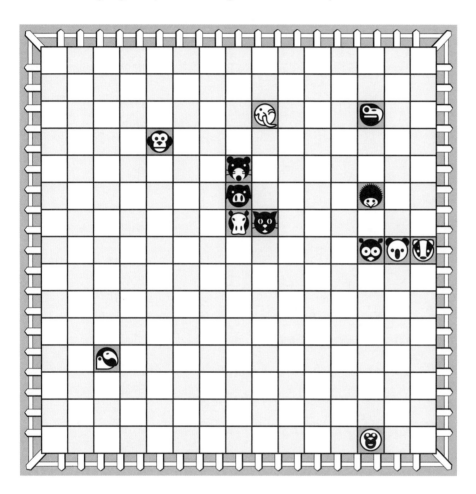

TRANSADDITION

Add one letter to letters from the words below and rearrange the rest to find a word that is related to the original phrase.

PERMEATING LIVING ROOM

★ Jazz

All the words listed are hidden vertically, horizontally or diagonally—in both directions. The letters that remain unused form a sentence from left to right.

```
J A D Z Z M U S N I D C O R I
A C I R F A G O I A P N A T E
N O I S U F T D V A O T T C H
S N A V E G N I W S B E B L E
E G I N N V S N I R E K R A P
U N G I O A A F T I B H E R T
L O L O S B W L P S E E N I T
B L I M E U T S S H E S C N E
E A O N T T E A T U R L Y E K
A N K M O L B Y D E O U I T C
K N G E L A A V R V J P S M E
S T D I R D A O A R N M U N B
R A G T I M E O H E A I G C U
E O N L R C I D N V B T N H R
E O O S T R S O I A A S I I B
C H O R D S A O E N I N M U E
R H Y T H M B T R U M P E T G
W O R B I G B A N D L E A N S
```

CLARINET
CONTRABASS
DAVIS
DRUGS
ELLINGTON
EVANS
FUSION
GILLESPIE
GUITAR
HOLIDAY
IMPULSE
MILES
MINGUS
MONK
PARKER
PIANO
RAGTIME
REINHARDT
RHYTHM
SLAVES
SOLO
SWING
TRUMPET
TUBA
VERVE
VOODOO

AFRICA
BAKER
BANJO

BASIE
BEBOP
BIG BAND

BLUES
BRUBECK
CHORDS

MISSING LETTER PROVERB

Fill in each missing letter, indicated by an X, to make a well-known proverb.

CLXAXLIXEXS IX NXXX XO XOXLIXEXS

★★ Bring Me Sunshine

The arrows below point in the direction of spots where the sun will shine, shown by the sun symbol. One spot is already shown. Can you locate the other spots? The sun symbols cannot adjoin each other vertically, horizontally or diagonally. A symbol cannot be placed on top of an arrow.

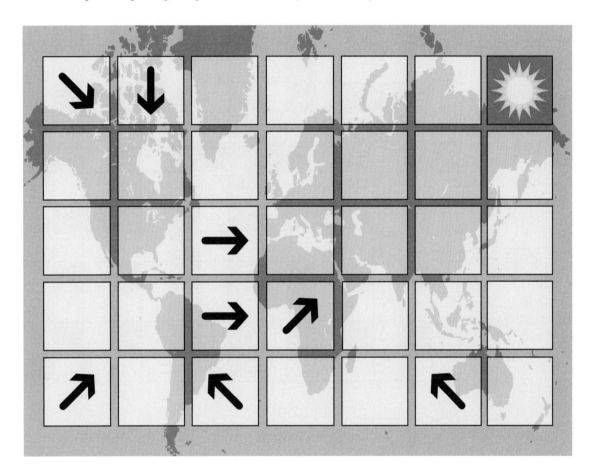

TAKE THE HINT

Use the letters from the word given in capital letters to form the words that are described in the brackets. Write your answer in the row of letter blocks. Four additional letters are already in place.

RINGBIRD (board on collapsible supports)

| | | O | | N | | | O | A | | |

★ Quick and Easy

ACROSS

1 Deep blue
5 Sugar snap
10 Child, juvenile
11 Brazilian dance
12 Malicious setting of fire
13 Religious community of brothers
14 Involve in intrigue or strife
16 Informal alliance
18 Sunshade
20 Housebreaker
22 Athos, Porthos or Aramis
24 Incorrect
26 Gas that screens the earth from ultraviolet radiation
27 Sitting with a leg either side
28 Breed of white spitz dog
29 Turkish capital

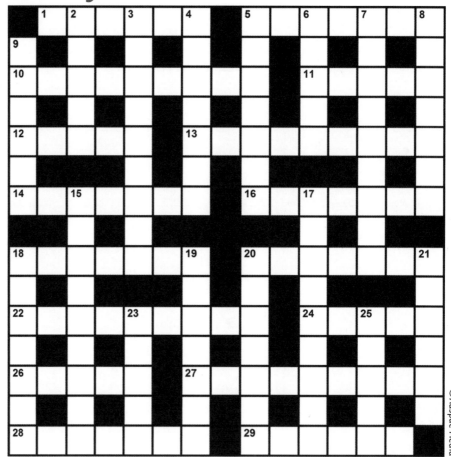

©Auspac Media

DOWN

2 Naming words
3 Cleverly inventive
4 Best, ideal
5 Hypodermic needle
6 Fertile spots in the desert
7 Herb with scarlet flowers
8 Break down and consider in detail
9 Spin, rotate
15 Tour rural areas on a political campaign
17 Reversion to an ancestral type
18 Pretentious, bombastic
19 The side away from the wind
20 Stiff cap worn by Catholic clergy
21 Rocky, rough
23 Paper used in polishing
25 Command

★ Kakuro

Each number in a black square is the sum of the numbers to be filled in the adjacent empty boxes. The empty boxes that make up the sum are called a run. The sum of the 'across run' is written above the diagonal in the black area, and the sum of the 'down run' is written below the diagonal. Runs can contain only the numbers 1 to 9 and each number in a run can be used only once. The grey boxes contain only odd numbers and the white only even numbers.

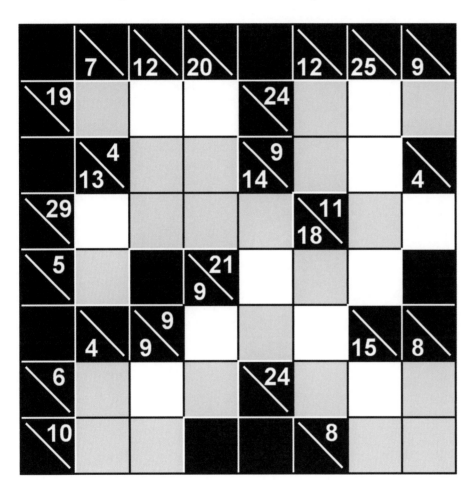

ONE LETTER LESS OR MORE

The word on the right side contains the letters of the word on the left side minus the letter shown in the middle. What is the word? One letter is already in the right place.

INCREASE -A- ☐ ☐ ☐ C ☐ ☐ ☐

★★★ BrainSnack®—Pedal Power

Which of the cycling gloves, numbered from 1 to 6, is the odd one out?

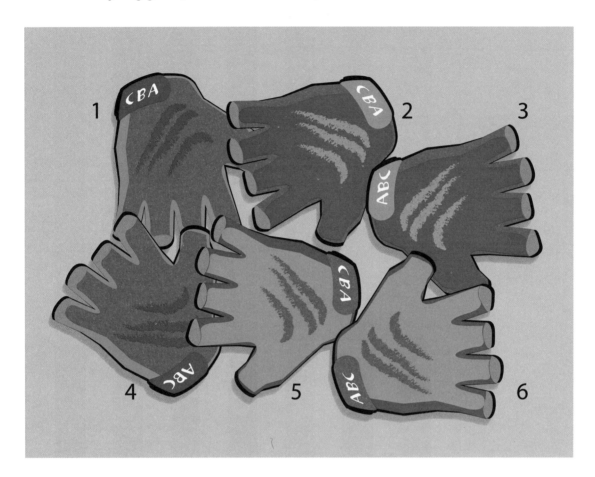

END GAME

The words you are seeking all have the letters END in them in the position indicated. When you have found all of the answers, from the clues on the right, one column will reveal the END GAME word but no need to go into it.

_	_	_	_	_	E	N	D		Share of profits
E	N	D	_	_	_	_	_		Finishing line
_	_	E	N	D	_	_	_		Mixing
_	E	N	D	_	_	_	_		Gently

★ Quick and Easy

ACROSS

1 Political and spiritual leader of Indian independence
5 Advance showing
10 Secluded corners
11 Doubt
12 Short, witty remark
13 Violent storm
14 Paying attention
17 Assumed name
18 Tumbler
20 Gradual increase in volume
22 Miser, cheapskate
24 Ceaseless
26 Specify as a condition of agreement
27 Bulbous vegetable
28 Training school
29 Place of worship

DOWN

2 Garlic mayonnaise
3 Merit, warrant
4 Someone who cannot sleep
5 Assert, propound
6 Former province of Ethiopia, now independent
7 Counterfeit
8 Looking at goods without buying (6,8)
9 The educated elite
15 Place of imagined peace and happiness (7-2)
16 Conservation zone around a city (5,4)
19 Height, standing
21 Adjust to accepted standards
23 Journal
25 Try out, test

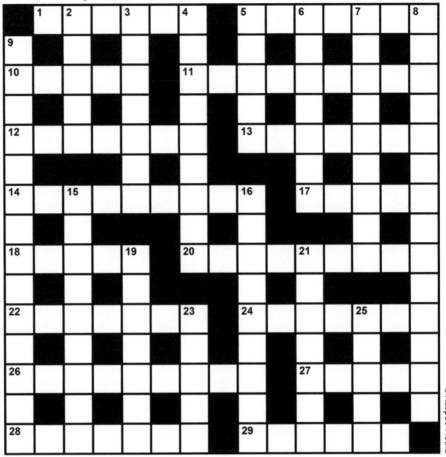

©Auspac Media

★★ Keep Going

Starting on a blank square of your choice, connect as many blank squares as possible with one single continuous line. You can only connect squares along vertical and horizontal lines, not along diagonal lines. You must continue the connecting line up until the next obstacle, i.e. the rim of the box, a black square or a square that has already been used. You can change direction at any obstacle you meet. Each square can be used only once. The number of blank squares that will be left unused is marked in the upper square. There is more than one solution. We show only one solution.

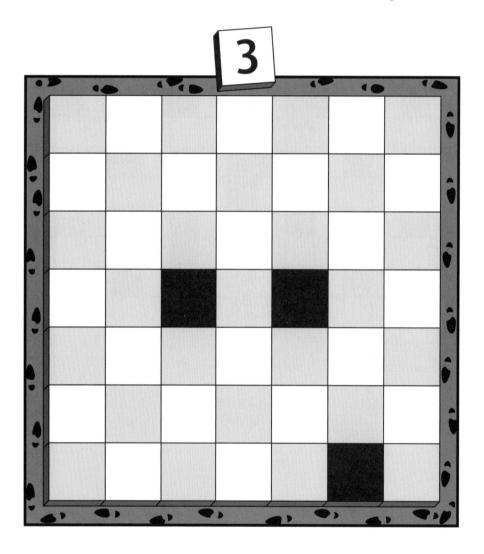

DELETE ONE

Delete one letter from BEATERS and rearrange the rest to get your money back.

★★★ Sudoku

Fill in the grid so that each row, each column and each 3 x 3 frame contains every number from 1 to 9.

	4						5	9
8			4					
			1		6	9		4
						7		8
2		3						
		4		8	1	6	9	7
7	8			3	9		4	1
9		1	2	4	7			3

SUMMER SCHOOL

Fill the boxes with the numbers 1 to 9 to give the correct row, column and diagonal totals.

		4	11
			19
			15
18	14	13	6

©Auspac Media

★ Circuit Breaker

How many words of 4 letters or more can you make from these 9 letters? In making a word each letter may be used only once, and the centre letter must be included. No slang, foreign words, hyphens, apostrophes, or plurals ending in 's'.
Source: Collins Dictionary

TARGET
GOOD 20; VERY GOOD 24; EXCELLENT 28; GENIUS 32

© Auspac Media

★★★ Sport Maze

Draw the shortest route from the golf ball to the hole. You can only move along vertical and horizontal lines, not along diagonal lines. The figure in each square indicates the number of squares the ball must be moved in the same direction. You can change directions at each stop. You can also retrace your path. The hole must be entered with the exact number of moves shown on the last square.

2	1	4	4	2	3
2	3	3	2	2	1
1	2	1	2	2	2
5	4	3	3	4	5
2	4	4	2	1	5
○	1	1	4	1	3

TAKE THE HINT

Use the letters from the word given in capital letters to form the words that are described in the brackets. Write your answer in the row of letter blocks. Three additional letters are already in place.

SENEGAL (U.S. city)

	O						L		S

★ Word Sudoku

Complete the grid so that each row, each column and each 3 x 3 frame contains the nine letters from the black box below. A nine-letter word is hidden in the diagonal from top left to bottom right.

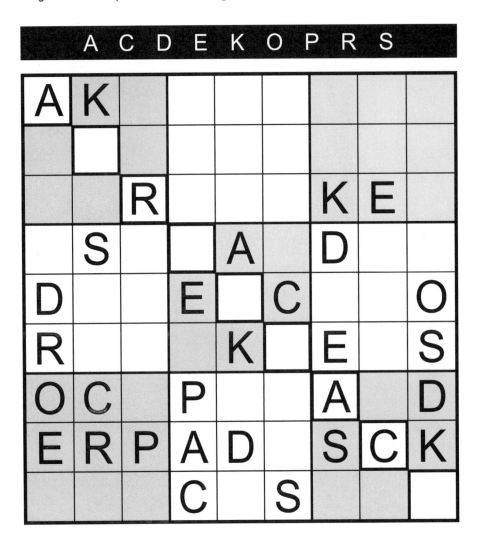

ONE LETTER LESS OR MORE

The word on the right side contains the letters of the word on the left side minus the letter in the middle. What is the word? One letter is already in the right place.

MAGAZINE -E ☐ ☐ ☐ Z ☐ ☐ ☐

★★★ BrainSnack®—Shirt Number

The number on each shirt is based on its combination of circles. Each colour represents a different value and, as with Roman numerals, a smaller value that precedes a larger value is deducted. Can you calculate the number that should replace the question mark on shirt 6?

UNCANNY TURN

Rearrange the letters of the words below to form a new word or phrase that is related to it in some way. The answer can be one or more words.

CLEAR SPICE PIE

★★ Teaser

ACROSS

3 Powder
6 Sets down heavily
9 Ten years
10 Nettlerash
11 Slender
12 Garment
13 Tyrannical person
15 Adder
16 Laid bare
17 Tree
20 Stretcher
22 Hackneyed
23 Advantage
27 Precious stone
28 Commerce
29 Barrier
30 Obtain
32 Kilns for drying hops
34 Makes level
37 Distinctive check
40 Silken
41 Widen
42 Linked series
43 Repaired
45 Affray
46 Timber-dressing tool
47 Tiny
48 Required
49 Condition
50 Cult

©Auspac Media

DOWN

1 Table-shaped hill
2 Vegetable
3 Wild ruffian
4 Shakes with cold
5 Faint-hearted
6 Find out
7 Taker of illegal interest
8 Confidential
13 Saves from possible loss
14 Monkey
18 Abstract
19 Stayed
21 Giggle
24 Briny
25 Newt
26 Will
31 Highest mountain
33 Cheat
35 Most agreeable
36 Plot
38 Consumed
39 Give up
41 Clock faces
44 Eternally

★ Cage the Animals

Draw the lines that will completely divide up the grid into smaller squares, representing cages, with exactly one animal per cage. Each cage can be as small as a single grid square. The cages cannot overlap.

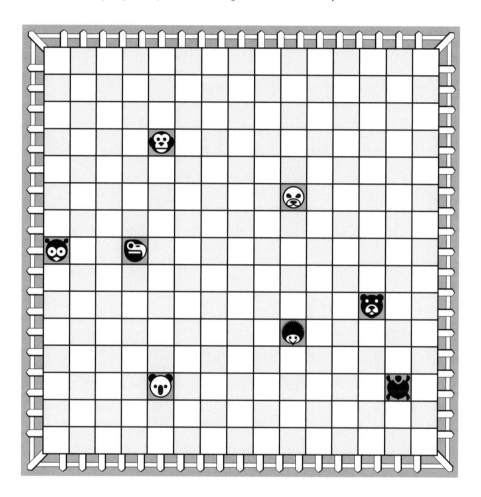

DOODLE PUZZLE

A doodle puzzle is a combination of images, letters and/or numbers that represent a word or a concept. If you cannot solve a doodle puzzle, do not look at the answer right away. Think hard—and outside the box.

5 down
4 down
3 down
2 down
1 down

★★ Binairo

Complete the grid with zeros and ones until there are five zeros (0) and six ones (1) in every row and every column. No more than two of the same number can be next to or under each other. Rows or columns with exactly the same content are not allowed. There is only one valid solution per puzzle.

						I				
I										
		I		I			O		O	
I		I		O						
				I			I	I		
			I	I		I				
					O				O	
		O		I	I					
	O			I				I		
			O						I	
O	I				O	O			I	

CHANGE ONE

Change one letter in each of these two words to form a common two-word phrase.

RUMBLE PIT

★★ Teaser

ACROSS

3 Gloomy
7 Relish
9 Snow leopard
10 Fondness
12 Distant
13 Repeat
15 Sky-coloured
17 Plunder
18 Taking in
21 First woman
23 Build
25 Teacher
27 Outline
28 Blemish
29 Building covering
30 Develops
33 Letting contracts
35 Ventilated
38 Sphere
39 Four-sided figure
42 Tree
44 Kingdom
45 Feeling of
   discomfort
47 Anger
48 Break suddenly
49 Call out
50 Air-passage
51 Cleats

DOWN

1 Find the place of
2 Suffer
3 Fault
4 Fragment
5 Fact of being
   elsewhere
6 Fate
7 Nothing
8 Seesaw
11 Springlike
14 Encourage in
   crime
16 Repeats from
   memory
19 As well
20 Leaves out
22 With great
   rapidity (mus.)
24 Long, slender
   sword
26 Meanly submissive
27 Non-verse
31 Obnoxious
   creatures
32 Fermentation
   vessel
33 Took shape
34 Biblical character
35 Concurs
36 Sanity
37 Bushman's bread
40 Pancake
41 Copying
43 Final
46 Tool

©Auspac Media

★ BrainSnack®—Autumn Colours

How many different types of trees are in the forest?

LETTER LINE

Each word below—paired with a set of numbers—is a clue to another word. This word will have the same number of letters as digits in its paired number. When you have found that word, match up each letter with its paired digit—the digit will tell you which square below in which to place the letter. When all the letters are in the correct squares, they will make a word that means 'to present or announce.' Example: Put a letter in each of the squares below to make a word which means 'delightful'. 841 BREACH; 762 NOTHING; 57613 BIRD. Answer: Gap; Nil; Snipe.

1	2	3	4	5	6	7	8
P	L	E	A	S	I	N	G

4 9 6 7 8 3 1 5 2 MONEY OFF; 1 2 6 7 8 9 PERSUADE;
8 5 2 6 7 1 3 PASSAGE; 4 7 1 2 9 6 DESTROYED.

1	2	3	4	5	6	7	8	9

★ Cars

All the words are hidden vertically, horizontally or diagonally—in both directions. The letters that remain unused form a sentence from left to right.

```
R I N C R D R A O B H S A D N
O E T A R S B U M P E R I N O
O W H E E L L G L G N I N U T
D H G Y D Y E S T R T R I M S
I E I D N S S C T E R U O E I
N E L O I V E C O U P É R H P
I L E B L N I K R C R O N B P
M S K E Y N D T A O L H A E O
L L A A C G W I T R A U D S F
M I R R O R A A C N B A T O R
C E B C A R I B D A L C M C A
N U F A C D T L R S T O U R H
E R S T A O E L O I O O K F O
S P A R K P L U G R A L R A L
T E R N A S T L E B T A E S T
I V T A E S K C A B E N S O U
R P M A L G O F C E S T O F E
N E T H E A D L I G H T R G Y
```

AIRBAG
BACK SEAT
BODY
BRAKE LIGHT
BRAKES
BUMPER
CLUTCH
COOLANT
COUPÉ
CYLINDER
DASHBOARD
DIESEL
DOOR
FOG LAMP
HANDLE
HEADLIGHT
HORN
INDICATORS
MIRROR
PEDALS
PISTON
RADIATOR
RIMS
SEAT
SEAT BELT
SPARK PLUG
TUNING
TURBO
WHEEL
WHEELS

FRIENDS

What same word or affix can be added to the following to make new words?

CURRICULAR GALACTICAL MARITAL ORDINARY SENSORY VASCULAR

★★ Teaser

ACROSS

1 Leave
5 Tear
9 Poet's Ireland
10 Wild excitement
12 Courageous
13 Tree
15 Obscure
16 That time
17 Condition
19 Argue
20 Ancient Roman days
21 Practical person
25 Anon
27 Beverage
28 Sacrificial table
30 Cosy retreats
32 Wrath
33 Social class
34 Printers' measures
36 Hindu garment
37 Small slabs
39 Cain's brother
42 Persist in pressing
45 Lofty structure
47 Principal
48 Insect
49 Before
50 Of the ear
51 Lump of gold
52 Yield
53 Flatters
54 Oppose

©Auspac Media

DOWN

2 Ooze out
3 Spicy fragrance
4 Seesaw
5 Generous
6 Soon
7 Extremities
8 Hackneyed
11 Tapes
13 Passing craze
14 Forcible control

18 Knighthoods
19 Preserve by drying
22 Blackboard support
23 Smallest amount
24 Droop
26 Stinging plant
29 Buying and selling
31 Briny

35 Threatens
38 Wrongdoer
40 Wearied with tediousness
41 Female sheep
43 Wise men
44 Slender supports
46 Roster
47 Rodents

★★ **Keep Going**

Starting on a blank square of your choice, connect as many blank squares as possible with one single continuous line. You can only connect squares along vertical and horizontal lines, not along diagonal lines. You must continue the connecting line up until the next obstacle, i.e. the rim of the box, a black square or a square that has already been used. You can change direction at any obstacle you meet. Each square can be used only once. The number of blank squares that will be left unused is marked in the upper square. There is more than one solution. We show only one solution.

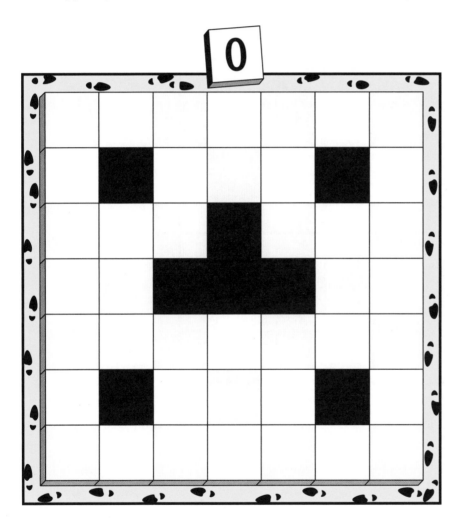

REPOSITION PREPOSITION

Unscramble the words below and find a three-word phrase.

OWN CHAIR ACCIDENT

_____ _____ _____

★★ Sudoku

Fill in the grid so that each row, each column and each 3 x 3 frame contains every number from 1 to 9.

	9			5	8	7		4
5	7	1		3	9	8		
6		4	1	2	7	5		
7		5				1		
4	1							9
		3						
		8		1				5
	4		7					
				9				

SANDWICH

What four-letter word belongs between the word at left and the word at right, so that the first and second word, and the second and third word, each form a common compound word?

FRIEND __ __ __ __ WRECK

★★ Teaser

ACROSS

3 Family members
7 Added clause
10 Inn
11 Waterway
12 Eastern couch
13 Joke
15 Wine
16 Common finch
17 Retributive justice
19 Decree
22 Sculptured likeness
25 Entrance
26 Leaked out
28 Break suddenly
30 Acting part
32 Heckled
34 Poet
36 Chemical compounds
38 Time in grammar
39 Ghost
42 Accompany for protection
44 Electrical unit
45 Make brown
46 Fastening
47 Of birth
48 Spiritualists' meeting
49 Discharge in disgrace
50 Card game

© Auspac Media

DOWN

1 Piled up
2 Mechanical flight
3 Fiery
4 Combine
5 Vestige
6 Wrongdoing
7 Record
8 Persia
9 Steal cattle
14 Insect
16 Speech defect
18 Meditated
20 Prescribed amounts
21 Lifting machine
23 Sun-dried brick
24 Consumers
27 Ward off
29 Confidential
31 Sources of light
33 Catch sight of
35 Blotted out
36 Pardon
37 Slight tinge
38 Frame of mind
40 Stringed instrument
41 Small civet
43 Weathercock
46 Headwear

★ Word Sudoku

Complete the grid so that each row, each column and each 3 x 3 frame contains the nine letters from the black box below. A nine-letter word is hidden in the diagonal from top left to bottom right.

B C E I O R T U W

	W				E			
B			R					
R		U			O			
					B			I
T					E	R		
				E			O	
O		B	E	W	U	I		
W	I			R		O		U
U			O	T		B	W	R

LETTERBLOCKS

Move the letter blocks around to form two words, one on the top line, the other on the bottom line, that are the names of musical instruments. Letters can be moved from one line to the other.

P G R P E B I
E U A M T T P

_ _ _ _ _ _ _

_ _ _ _ _ _ _ _

★★★ Sport Maze

Draw the shortest route from the golf ball to the hole. You can only move along vertical and horizontal lines, not along diagonal lines. The figure in each square indicates the number of squares the ball must be moved in the same direction. You can change directions at each stop. You can also retrace your path. The hole must be entered with the exact number of moves shown on the last square.

1	5	3	4	4	4
1	2	○	4	2	1
4	3	3	1	4	4
4	2	1	3	4	2
1	2	4	3	1	4
2	1	5	4	1	2

DOUBLETALK

What six-letter word means 'a thing' or 'to protest'?

— — — — — —

★★ Teaser

ACROSS

1 Capsize
4 Involving two sides
8 Lyric poem
10 Courage
11 Cover
13 Large building
14 Flattened spoon
15 Quote
16 Fish traps
19 Go before
22 Gage
25 Tricks
26 Govern
27 Cicatrice
29 Chinese
31 Ineffectual
32 Defend
33 Waistband
36 Annoying child
39 Suffocated in liquid
42 Flatter
43 Golf mound
44 Sing as a Tyrolean mountaineer
45 Everyone
46 Yield
47 Comforted

©Auspac Media

DOWN

1 Invisible
2 Allowing no laxity
3 Strengthening medicine
4 Headwear
5 Liquor dregs
6 Send out
7 Finds the place of
9 Unit of noise intensity

11 Belonging to the side
12 Low sand hills
17 Young eel
18 Spar set diagonally (naut.)
19 Nuisance
20 Remedies
21 Notches
23 Alfalfa
24 Clever in movement

28 City fortress
29 Arachnids
30 Mechanical man
34 Astounds
35 Paid attention
37 Radiolocation
38 Delicate fabric
40 Have on
41 Stained

★★★ BrainSnack®—Star Gazer

Which of the stars, numbered from 1 to 12, is not the correct colour?

TRANSADDITION

Add one letter to letters from the words below and rearrange the rest to find a word that is related to the original phrase.

TRAILS NUT

★ Sudoku Twin

Fill in the grid so that each row, each column and each 3 x 3 frame contains every number from 1 to 9. A sudoku twin is two connected 9 x 9 sudokus.

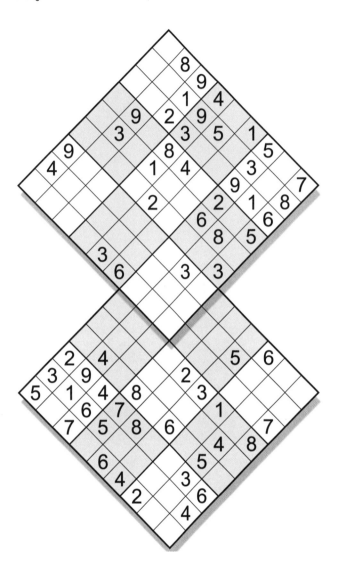

TAKE THE HINT

Use the letters from the words given in capital letters to form the word that is described in the brackets. Write your answer in the row of letter blocks. One additional letter is already in the right place.

CANNOT CUT (someone who audits business)

A								

★★ Teaser

ACROSS
3 Understand
9 Over
10 Spirit
11 Representative
14 Dealer
17 Man's name
20 Alone
21 Dash
22 Consumed
23 Lustre
25 Matures
26 Concise
27 Join the army
29 Ailments
31 Mine opening
32 Come forward
36 Permission
38 Make fast a vessel
39 Lofty structure
41 Hawaiian dish
42 Direction
43 Newts
46 Spread
   stragglingly
48 Salad item
50 Being monarch
51 Command
52 Hanging

©Auspac Media

DOWN
1 Endures
2 Oral
3 Yield
4 Balk
5 Floor covering
6 Arose
7 Water pitcher
8 Widens
12 Celtic tongue
13 Weight
15 Acting part

16 Brief
18 Wise Men (Bib.)
19 Settle cosily
24 Grasped
25 Changed
26 Vagrants
28 African river
30 Make lawful
33 Tub and cask
   makers
34 Coconut husk
   fibre

35 Made musical
37 Fermentation
   vessels
40 Caution
42 Female sheep
44 Discovers
45 Keen-edged
47 Weapons
49 In excited
   eagerness

★★ Bring Me Sunshine

The arrows below point in the direction of spots where the sun will shine, shown by the sun symbol. One spot is already shown. Can you locate the other spots? The sun symbols cannot adjoin each other vertically, horizontally or diagonally. A symbol cannot be placed on top of an arrow.

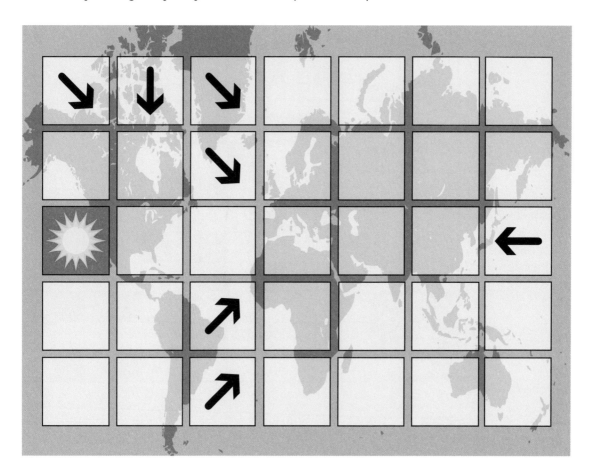

TAKE THE HINT

Use the letters from the words given in capital letters to form the words that are described in the brackets. Write your answer in the row of letter blocks. Two additional letters are already in the right place.

POOL TABLE FLY *(athlete)*

☐ ☐ ☐ ☐ ☐ **A** ☐ ☐   ☐ ☐ ☐ ☐ ☐ **R**

★ Word Pyramid

Each word in the pyramid is composed of the letters of the word above it, plus an additional letter. You can change the order of the letters as you make a new word.

A
(1) Babylonian god of wisdom
(2) large body of salt water
(3) occasion for buying at reduced prices
(4) rent
(5) benumbed
(6) get worse
(7) delight

MISSING LETTER PROVERB

Fill in each missing letter, indicated by an X, to make a well-known proverb.

XLX XOOX XXINXS MXST XOME XO AX XND

★ Cage the Animals

Draw the lines that will completely divide up the grid into smaller squares, representing cages, with exactly one animal per cage. Each cage can be as small as a single grid square. The cages cannot overlap.

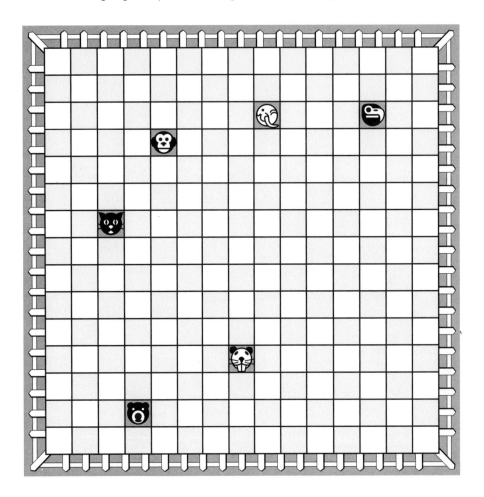

END GAME

The words you are seeking all have the letters END in them in the position indicated. When you have found all of the answers, from the clues on the right, one column will reveal the END GAME word and give you a shade.

```
_ _ _ E N D _ _      Meant
_ _ _ E N D _ _      Sociable
_ E N D _ _ _ _      Flexible
_ _ _ E N D _ _      Abandoned
```

★★ Teaser

ACROSS

3 Water grass
6 Underwater worker
9 Give to charity
10 Lowest point
11 At hand
12 Sound reasoning
13 Gallery of shops
15 Started
16 Magnates
17 Lukewarm
20 Salt lake
22 Draw out
23 Prescribed amounts
27 Corded cloth
28 Rescued
29 Respiratory organs
30 Make lace
32 Looks for
34 Turn inside out
37 Talking bird
40 Restaurant car
41 Slope backward
42 Watery part of blood
43 Persuaded by flattery
45 Play unskilfully
46 Fine sediment
47 Church cantata
48 Foreign-looking
49 Command
50 Transmit

DOWN

1 Needy
2 Smallgoods item
3 Apostates
4 Makes possible
5 Ventures
6 Widen
7 Pressed clothes
8 Large building
13 Helped
14 Spanish nobleman
18 Ship's officer
19 Portrayed
21 Pay attention
24 Lyric poem
25 Large deer
26 Mistrusted
31 Pilot
33 Recluse
35 Begin again
36 Vibration
38 Fuss
39 Sanity
41 Tricks
44 Way out

© Auspac Media

★ Binairo

Complete the grid with zeros and ones until there are six zeros (0) and six ones (1) in every row and every column. No more than two of the same number can be next to or under each other. Rows or columns with exactly the same content are not allowed. There is only one valid solution per puzzle.

	0		0								
0			1						1		
	0				1		0				
			0		1					0	0
	1	1					1		0		
0	1							1			
						0					
	1		1		1		0		1		0
	0	0				1		1	1		1
		1		1		0		1	1		1

LETTER LINE

Each word below—paired with a set of numbers—is a clue to another word. This word will have the same number of letters as digits in its paired number. When you have found that word, match up each letter with its paired digit—the digit will tell you which square below in which to place the letter. When all the letters are in the correct squares, they will make a word that means 'to take from.'

1 8 4 10 COFFEE SHOP; 9 2 3 5 1 6 PICK ME UPS;
4 8 7 10 9 6 ASPECTS; 7 2 3 7 5 6 10 SHORT.

1	2	3	4	5	6	7	8	9	10

★★ Keep Going

Starting on a blank square of your choice, connect as many blank squares as possible with one single continuous line. You can only connect squares along vertical and horizontal lines, not along diagonal lines. You must continue the connecting line up until the next obstacle, i.e. the rim of the box, a black square or a square that has already been used. You can change direction at any obstacle you meet. Each square can be used only once. The number of blank squares that will be left unused is marked in the upper square. There is more than one solution. We show only one solution.

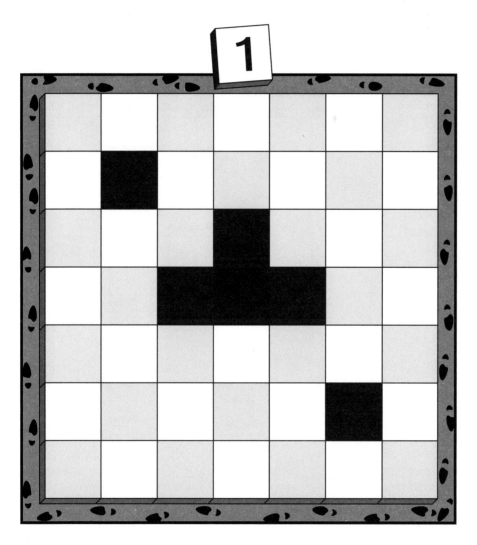

DELETE ONE

Delete one letter from INSTANCES and rearrange the rest to find elders.

★★ Teaser

ACROSS

3 Mythical monster
7 Electric insulator
9 Nimble
10 Bundle
12 As well
13 Serial part
15 Senseless
17 Make brown
18 Will
21 Incision
23 Summit
25 Changes
27 Speech defect
28 Gem
29 Part of the eye
30 Dispossessed by law
33 Looked after
35 Assail
38 Anger
39 Elastic
42 Goal
44 Coral isle
45 Keep out of enjoyment
47 Vigour
48 Soon
49 Banishment
50 Precipitation
51 Married

©Auspac Media

DOWN

1 Lunatic
2 Sea-robber
3 Hate intensely
4 Spicy fragrance
5 Abnormally fat
6 Short sleep
7 Table-shaped hill
8 Wards off
11 Small
14 Single occasion

16 Settled cosily
19 Extinct bird
20 Nominated
22 Bearlike
24 Long, slender sword
26 Three-pronged spear
27 Move easily
31 Obnoxious creatures
32 Prefix-three

33 Dry inflammable matter
34 Tide of smallest range
35 Smiled radiantly
36 Impassive
37 Bank employee
40 View
41 Black and blue
43 Persia
46 Solemn promise

★★★ BrainSnack®—Seedless

One hundred per cent pure Burgundian grape juice, made from grape pulp, consists of the following percentages of water, sugars, tannin, acids, cellulose and minerals in order from top to bottom. Which percentage is wrong?

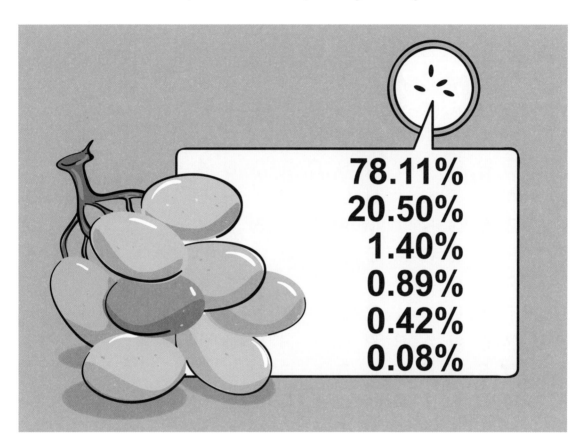

78.11%
20.50%
1.40%
0.89%
0.42%
0.08%

SQUIRCLES

Place consonants in the squares and vowels in the circles to form words in each vertical column. The definitions of the words you are looking for are listed. (The grid will reveal the names of two animals.)

1 Give away
2 Nut
3 Expose to air
4 First event
5 Cold
6 Vote
7 Not fully developed
8 Engraved

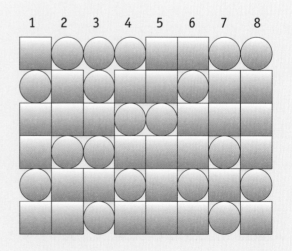

★ Mathematics

All the words are hidden vertically, horizontally or diagonally—in both directions. The letters that remain unused form a sentence from left to right.

```
N I N M O S T E L A N G U A G
A E E S T S H E D A W O T R D
R F V O R M C A X I T H I E M
B A N E G A T I V E V T G I C
E S I R R S O E T D N I I E R
G I C E E M V V N S O E D D A
L D I W T F R I U O I M T H E
A C G O E G R T M A T T E E K
B W O P M L O A B B C R A R D
O S L S A C L V E A U I M T L
D Á U T I H I I R C D A N A S
Y È M R D N A R P U E N R O W
P R O O F H E E C S D G A I C
C M A R G A I D H L E L E M E
M A T R I X C A N T E E N S S
C I E X P O N E N T N E I N C
E K N Y T I N I F N I O L W L
E D G E O R L E A R L N I N G
```

ABACUS
ADD
ALGEBRA
AXIOM
BODY
CIRCLE
CONIC
COSINE
DEDUCTION
DERIVATIVE
DIAGRAM
DIAMETER
DIGIT
DIVIDE
ELLIPSE
EVEN
EXPONENT
INFINITY
INTEGRAL
LINE
LINEAR
LOGIC
MATRIX
NEGATIVE
NUMBER
POWER
PROOF
STATISTICS
SURFACE
TRIANGLE

ONE LETTER LESS OR MORE

The word on the right side contains the letters of the word on the left side plus the letter in the middle. What is the word? One letter is already in the right place.

C A N O E I N G +R ☐ ☐ N ☐ ☐ ☐ ☐ ☐

★★ Circuit Breaker

How many words of 4 letters or more can you make from these 9 letters? In making a word each letter may be used only once, and the centre letter must be included. No slang, foreign words, hyphens, apostrophes, or plurals ending in 's'.
Source: Collins Dictionary

TARGET
GOOD 23; VERY GOOD 30; EXCELLENT 37; GENIUS 44

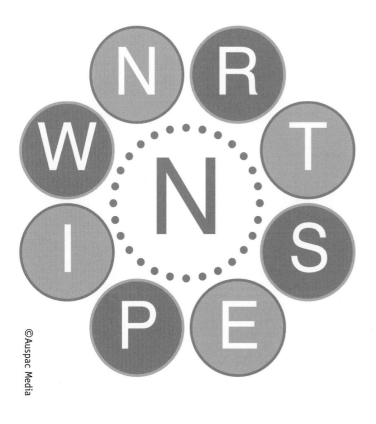

©Auspac Media

★★ Number Cluster

Complete the grid by forming adjoining clusters that consist of as many cubes as the number shown on the cubes. At cube 5, for example, you will have to make a cluster of five adjoining cubes. The number already shown in a cube is counted as part of the cluster. You can only place your cubes along horizontal and/or vertical lines, never diagonally.

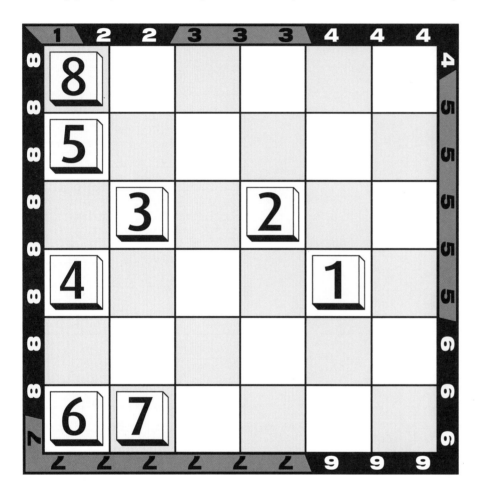

UNCANNY TURN

Rearrange the letters of the words below to form a new word or phrase that is related to it in some way. The answer can be one or more words.

HEAR SET

★★ BrainSnack®—Skewered

A sausage costs half as much as a meatball, and a beef cube costs twice as much as a meatball. The entire package costs $16.20. How much does a sausage cost?

DOODLE PUZZLE

A doodle puzzle is a combination of images, letters and/or numbers that represent a word or a concept. If you cannot solve a doodle puzzle, do not look at the answer right away. Think hard—and outside the box.

★★ Teaser

ACROSS

1 Envious
5 Facial hair
9 Chatters
10 Aristocratic
11 Speak publicly
12 Of the beach
13 Re-adjust
15 Painting support
17 Pallid
20 Pen tip
21 Lubricant
23 Curved (roof)
27 Small fruit
30 Statistics chart
32 Daunt
33 Nuzzled
34 Approaches
35 Green gem
36 Naturists
37 Withstood

DOWN

1 Woodworkers
2 Suspects' excuses
3 Item
4 Underground
   railroads
5 Grapple
6 Shoe lining
7 Works (dough)
8 Revokes (law)
14 Glowing coal

16 Scent
17 Also
18 Garment edge
19 Show agreement
22 Leave behind
24 Corkscrews

25 Arise (from)
26 Dined well
28 Grated
29 Sings alpine-style
30 Minded
31 Bringer (of news)

©Lovatts Puzzles

★★★ Sport Maze

Draw the shortest route from the golf ball to the hole. You can only move along vertical and horizontal lines, not along diagonal lines. The figure in each square indicates the number of squares the ball must be moved in the same direction. You can change directions at each stop. You can also retrace your path. The hole must be entered with the exact number of moves shown on the last square.

1	4	5	5	4	4
2	4	4	2	4	2
4	1	3	2	4	4
1	4	2	3	○	5
1	2	1	4	3	3
3	4	3	5	4	3

CHANGE ONE

Change one letter in each of these two words to form a common two-word phrase.

GREED BINGERS

★ Word Sudoku

Complete the grid so that each row, each column and each 3 x 3 frame contains the nine letters from the black box below. The hidden nine-letter word is in the diagonal from top left to bottom right.

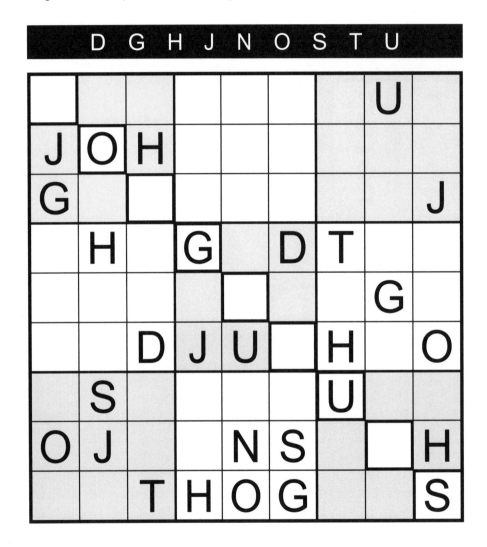

LETTERBLOCKS

Move the letter blocks around to form two words, one on the top line, the other on the bottom line, that can be associated with gardens.

_ _ _ _ _ _ _ _

_ _ _ _ _ _ _ _

★★ Teaser

ACROSS

1 Arrives at
5 True-to-life quality
9 Standing on hind legs
10 Dough ingredient
11 Fill with joy
12 Taller
13 Light push
15 Barely sufficient
17 Wise saying
20 Animal exhibition
21 Decompose
23 Overweight
27 Harvests
30 Committing perjury
32 Mime
33 Fine display
34 Ladies
35 Added up
36 Auburn-haired person
37 Bashfulness

DOWN

1 Depending
2 Scared
3 Rush headlong
4 Provided with personnel
5 Hoisting (flag)
6 Annoys
7 Large lizard
8 Souvenir
14 Collection
16 Indian dish
17 In the past
18 Grow older
19 Preceding day
22 Mightier
24 Fought rowdily
25 Skin mite rash
26 Sufferings
28 Concurred
29 Grain-cutting tool
30 Indecently
31 Resistant to infection

©Lovatts Puzzles

★★★ Sudoku

Fill in the grid so that each row, each column and each 3 x 3 frame contains
every number from 1 to 9.

5		2	4	6	8		3	
			9		3		4	2
3					2			
6		7	2		9			8
2		4		7		3		
		3	8					7
	9	3						
7						5		
			8			6		

FRIENDS

What same word or affix can be added to the following to make new words?

BASE GRAM METER PAUSE
PHONE STOLE TRIBE

★★★ BrainSnack®—Multiplier

Assuming the answers of the previous multiplications are correct, what is the answer of the last calculation?

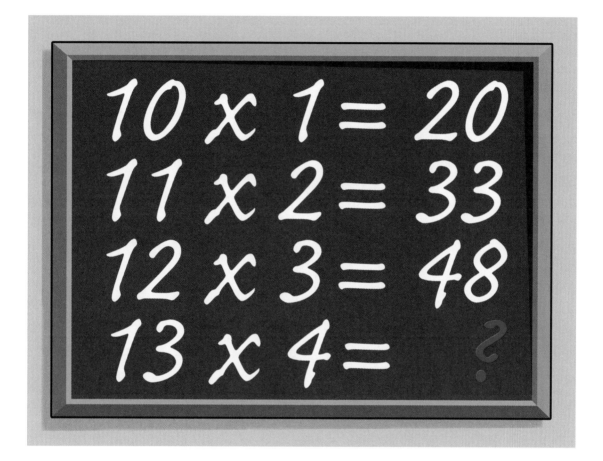

SANDWICH

What five-letter word belongs between the word at left and the word at right, so that the first and second word, and the second and third word, each form a common compound word?

FINGER _ _ _ _ _ MAKER

★★ Teaser

ACROSS

1 Predicament
5 Irritates
9 Entitling
10 Confused babble
12 Hoisting
13 Chapter heading
14 Highly curious
16 Graceful
19 Scuffled
21 Adorable
24 Stare angrily
25 Complaints arbiter
27 Finger-shaped pastry
28 Urge
29 Brutal person
30 Adopted (policy)

DOWN

1 Lined up
2 Astounds
3 River-mouth flats
4 Leasing
6 Most loyal
7 Customary
8 Topics
11 Storybook monster
15 Art museums
17 Stumbles wearily
18 Attacked

20 Entryway
21 Spider traps
22 Smudges
23 Mean (to)
26 1970s dance music

© Lovatts Puzzles

★ Spot the Differences

There are nine differences between these two images. Can you find them?
Circle the differences on the image on the right.

LETTERBLOCKS

Move the letter blocks around to form two words, one on the top line, the other on the bottom line, that can be associated with mistakes. Letters can be moved from one line to the other.

| R | L | U | B | N | D | E |

_ _ _ _ _ _ _

| R | L | O | B | O | P | E |

_ _ _ _ _ _ _

★★ Binairo

Complete the grid with zeros and ones until there are five zeros (0) and six ones (1) in every row and every column. No more than two of the same number can be next to or under each other. Rows or columns with exactly the same content are not allowed. There is only one valid solution per puzzle.

0				0						
	0		0							
1							0	0		
		1				0				
1				0		0			0	
							1			
	0		0						0	
				0			0			
	1					1				
	1		0			1		1		
	1			1				0		

DOUBLETALK

What seven-letter word means 'a topic' or 'to cause to undergo'?

— — — — — — —

★ Cage the Animals

Draw the lines that will completely divide up the grid into smaller squares, representing cages, with exactly one animal per cage. Each cage can be as small as a single grid square. The cages cannot overlap.

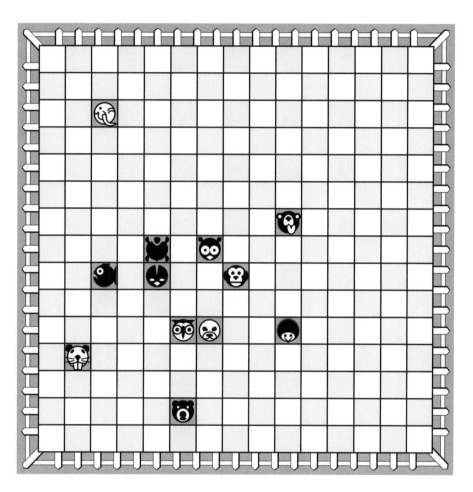

REPOSITION PREPOSITION

Unscramble HALF OF BONE and find a three-word phrase.

_____   _____   _____

★★ Teaser

ACROSS

- **1** Alpine landslides
- **6** Long tale
- **10** Covering for feet
- **11** Frightens
- **12** Scold
- **14** Segment
- **16** Attacking savagely
- **18** Submarine missile
- **20** Boarders
- **22** Hand bomb
- **23** Certify (accounts)
- **25** Earphone units
- **28** Grown-up stage
- **29** Show as similar
- **31** Level
- **32** Increasing in intensity

DOWN

- **1** As well
- **2** Circle part
- **3** Donkeys
- **4** Slicing
- **5** Heartfelt
- **7** Group of lions
- **8** Stews
- **9** Scatter
- **13** Hunting dog
- **15** Combine
- **17** Character
- **19** Precise
- **21** Learning institutes
- **22** Mum's mum
- **24** Drench
- **26** Spicy Mexican sauce
- **27** Warm and protected
- **30** Ornamental carp

©Lovatts Puzzles

★ Invest

All the words are hidden vertically, horizontally or diagonally—in both directions. The letters that remain unused form a sentence from left to right.

```
E  T  A  T  S  W  H  E  E  D  A  R  T  S  A
N  S  A  W  I  N  V  E  S  T  M  E  N  T  N
V  I  T  R  A  C  K  I  N  G  H  N  G  O  A
C  O  V  E  R  R  A  T  I  O  B  G  A  C  L
S  E  C  I  R  P  R  E  F  F  O  O  I  K  Y
E  Y  T  I  L  I  T  A  L  O  V  S  N  R  S
L  C  I  S  N  I  R  T  N  I  N  H  D  U  I
L  A  T  I  P  A  C  C  I  T  N  A  V  E  S
X  E  D  N  I  E  C  I  R  P  E  R  A  H  S
S  U  O  N  D  T  I  N  N  A  G  E  W  E  C
N  R  T  P  E  E  E  P  O  D  S  U  T  D  U
R  O  R  O  T  D  P  U  I  T  E  H  N  G  S
U  N  E  B  M  I  I  O  S  O  B  X  O  I  T
T  E  A  N  A  E  O  V  S  Y  F  O  D  N  O
E  X  S  S  O  N  R  N  I  I  A  F  N  G  D
R  T  U  E  D  E  K  T  M  D  T  H  O  D  I
E  R  R  E  B  A  Y  R  E  R  A  E  L  C  A
R  U  Y  N  N  I  Q  N  G  A  R  I  S  K  N
```

ANALYSIS
BANK
BOND
BONUS
CAPITAL
CLEARER
COVER RATIO
CRASH
CUSTODIAN
DEPOSIT
DIVIDEND
EMISSION
EURONEXT
HEDGING
INDEX
INTRINSIC
INVESTMENT
LONDON
NASDAQ
OFFER PRICE
OPTION
RETURN
RIGHT
SELL
SHARE
SHARE PRICE INDEX
STATE
STOCK
TRACKING
TRADE
TREASURY
VOLATILITY
WARRANT

TRANSADDITION

Add one letter to letters from the words below and rearrange the rest to find a word that is related to the original phrase.

RENAMING REVEALS

_____

★★ Bring Me Sunshine

The arrows below point in the direction of spots where the sun will shine, shown by the sun symbol. One spot is already shown. Can you locate the other spots? The sun symbols cannot adjoin each other vertically, horizontally or diagonally. A symbol cannot be placed on top of an arrow.

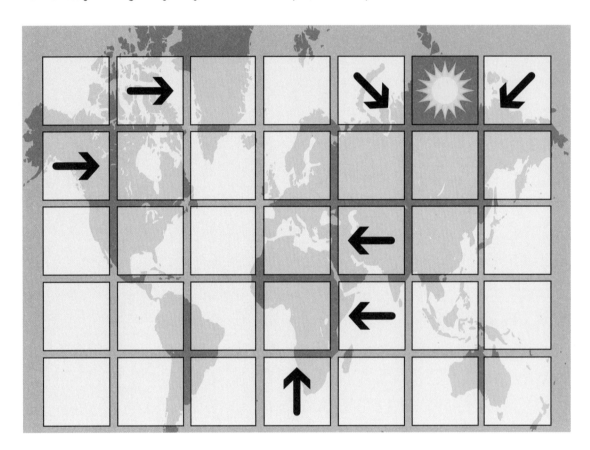

TAKE THE HINT

Use the letters from the words given in capitals to form the words that are described in the brackets. Write your answer in the row of letter blocks. One additional letter is already in place.

LONESOME RIG (chamber)

			P							

★★ Teaser

ACROSS

1 Theatrical
5 Funeral service speech
9 Lacking energy
10 Traffic light or flare
12 Church musicians
13 Eightsome
14 Sets of tools
16 Tasted
19 Unbranded (product)
21 Betting chances
24 Take (revenge)
25 Not temporary
27 Gold bricks
28 Smudging
29 Ravenous
30 Meant

DOWN

1 Serving (of cream)
2 Allocate
3 Actor, Woody ___
4 Demands
6 Wearing official dress
7 Elaborately
8 Christmas season
11 Requests
15 Annoyed
17 Going along (with)
18 Unknot
20 Sleeveless coat
21 Male rower
22 At the rear of
23 Put on (play)
26 Mindful

©Lovatts Puzzles

★★ BrainSnack®—Write One

Which letter should replace the question mark?

END GAME

The words you are seeking all have the letters END in them in the position indicated. When you have found all of the answers, from the clues on the right, one column will reveal the END GAME word which is an end game in itself.

_	_	_	_	_	E	N	D	Squander
	_	_	E	N	D	_	_	_	Cruel, wicked
	_	E	N	D	_	_	_	_	Available as a resource
E	N	D	_	_	_	_	_	Inner layers of cells

★★ Kakuro

Each number in a black square is the sum of the numbers to be filled in the adjacent empty boxes. The empty boxes that make up the sum are called a run. The sum of the 'across run' is written above the diagonal in the black area, and the sum of the 'down run' is written below the diagonal. Runs can contain only the numbers 1 to 9 and each number in a run can be used only once. The grey boxes contain only odd numbers and the white only even numbers.

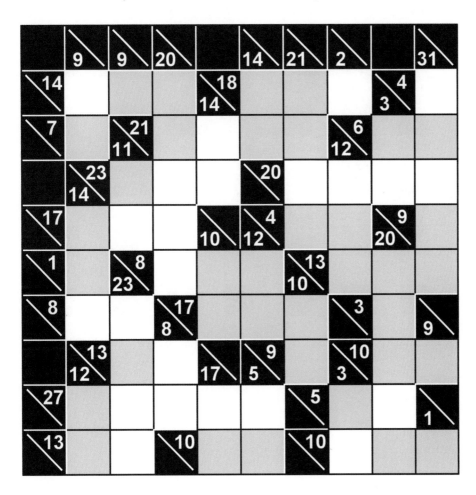

MISSING LETTER PROVERB

Fill in each missing letter, indicated by an X, to make a well-known proverb.

XAXKING XOXS XELXOM XITX

★★ Teaser

ACROSS

1 Costume jewellery
5 Guanaco relative
9 Ancestor
10 Split
12 Glazed
13 Become liable for
14 Linear network
16 Throes
19 Navigation aid
21 Thin layer of paint
24 Friendlier
25 Sanctions
27 Rebellion
28 Italian bread
29 Moves laterally
30 Increases in gradient

DOWN

1 Clash
2 Overseas
3 Saunter
4 Used dragnet
6 Confections
7 Lawless
8 Blood vessel swelling
11 Conception
15 Transpose
17 Earthquake waves
18 Carried out
20 Asian cuisine
21 Surfboard fall
22 Unsophisticated
23 Attempts
26 Egg-shaped

©Lovatts Puzzles

★★ Word Sudoku

Complete the grid so that each row, each column and each 3 x 3 frame contains the nine letters from the black box below. The hidden nine-letter-word is in the diagonal from top left to bottom right.

A B E R S T U W Y

T								
			B	W				
							S	
E	Y							
	A					R	B	
	R	Y				A		
S				T				W
R	U	S	W	B	A			
W	B	E	A	U	T			

LETTERBLOCKS

Move the letter blocks around to form two words, one on the top line, the other on the bottom line, that can be associated with emotions. Letters can be moved from one line to the other.

I H R E S P A
U D L O P E F

_ _ _ _ _ _ _

_ _ _ _ _ _ _

★★ Keep Going

Starting on a blank square of your choice, connect as many blank squares as possible with one single continuous line. You can only connect squares along vertical and horizontal lines, not along diagonal lines. You must continue the connecting line up until the next obstacle, i.e. the rim of the box, a black square or a square that has already been used. You can change direction at any obstacle you meet. Each square can be used only once. The number of blank squares that will be left unused is marked in the upper square. There is more than one solution. We show only one solution.

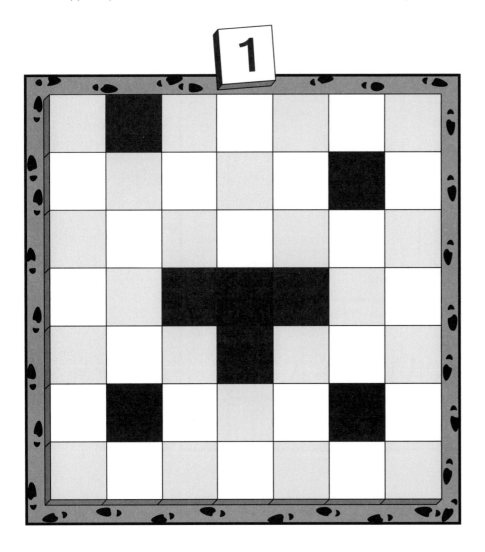

DELETE ONE

Delete one letter from USE ARMS A LOT and rearrange the rest to find a tumble.

★★ Teaser

ACROSS
- **1** Soap and candle maker
- **5** Tessellated picture
- **9** Fuse together
- **10** Comfort
- **12** Hospital workers
- **13** Put up
- **14** Plug
- **16** Sugar
- **19** Elusive
- **21** Sagacious
- **24** Endorses
- **25** Silos
- **27** Legal clerk
- **28** Annexed
- **29** Arbitrate
- **30** Circular storms

DOWN
- **1** Nest-stealing bird
- **2** Confers
- **3** Dismal
- **4** Inscribing
- **6** Distance gauges
- **7** Almond-flavoured liqueur
- **8** Generating
- **11** Quizzes
- **15** Without liability cover
- **17** Deplored
- **18** Of the Milky Way
- **20** Fabergé masterpieces
- **21** Prosperous
- **22** Rock growth
- **23** Digressions
- **26** Benefit

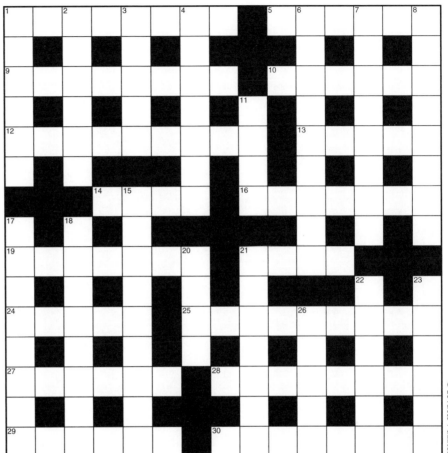

©Lovatts Puzzles

★★★ Sport Maze

Draw the shortest route from the golf ball to the hole. You can only move along vertical and horizontal lines, not along diagonal lines. The figure in each square indicates the number of squares the ball must be moved in the same direction. You can change directions at each stop. You can also retrace your path. The hole must be entered with the exact number of moves shown on the last square.

2	1	3	4	5	2
5	2	4	2	2	5
4	2	3	2	1	4
4	3	2	3	4	1
3	3	1	3	2	
3	1	5	2	3	2

LETTER LINE

Each word below—paired with a set of numbers—is a clue to another word. This word will have the same number of letters as digits in its paired number. When you have found that word, match up each letter with its paired digit—the digit will tell you which square below in which to place the letter. When all the letters are in the correct squares, they will make a word that means 'to found.'

8 3 4 5 6 1 STEADFAST; 5 4 2 7 6 HERB;
2 4 6 3 SEASONING; 8 6 4 5 CHUNK.

1	2	3	4	5	6	7	8	9

★★★ Sudoku

Fill in the grid so that each row, each column and each 3 x 3 frame contains every number from 1 to 9.

8								
	9	1						
7							4	2
		2	4					
4				9			1	8
				1	6			
		3		6	4		9	
	1		8		9	2	5	
	4	8	5	2		6	3	

SUMMER SCHOOL

Fill the boxes with the numbers 1 to 9 to give the correct row, column and diagonal totals.

			14
	5		14
			17
14	10	21	14

©Auspac Media

★★★ BrainSnack®—Kisses

Which letter should replace the question mark?

ONE LETTER LESS OR MORE

The word on the right side contains the letters of the word on the left side plus the letter in the middle. What is the word? One letter is already in the right place.

G R E N A D E S +E ☐ ☐ ☐ ☐ G ☐ ☐ ☐ ☐

★★ Teaser

ACROSS

1 Sliding snow masses
6 Fragrant salve
10 Affray
11 Rambled
12 Unnerves
14 Break (off)
16 Power cuts
18 Most intense
20 Pinto
22 Mediterranean rice dish
23 Economical
25 Mounted bullfighters
28 Gain
29 Infuse
31 Wide interval
32 Vulnerable to attack

DOWN

1 Charity offerings
2 Fully
3 Asserts
4 Coerces
5 Passed
7 Be consistent with
8 Temperance
9 Expeditions
13 Lissom
15 Condensing
17 Struggles
19 Type in
21 Push down
22 Cheese made from whey
24 Outdo
26 Sturdy cotton fabric
27 Scant
30 Plumb line weight

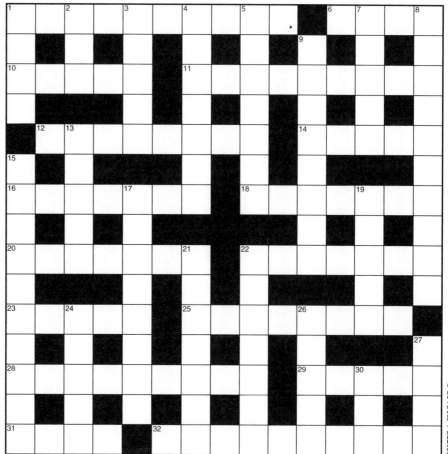

©Lovatts Puzzles

★ Biology

All the words are hidden vertically, horizontally or diagonally—in both directions. The letters that remain unused form a sentence from left to right.

```
B  S  I  O  E  S  U  G  N  U  F  L  S  O  G
Y  C  I  S  R  A  N  K  E  X  A  G  C  T  S
C  I  A  F  O  I  E  I  N  C  N  E  T  H  A
T  T  I  O  V  C  S  N  S  I  S  O  M  S  O
S  E  R  S  I  E  T  S  R  Y  L  I  M  A  F
D  N  E  S  N  L  U  H  Y  M  O  T  A  N  A
O  E  T  I  M  L  T  I  L  U  N  G  S  I  D
P  G  C  L  O  W  I  P  E  S  L  I  V  T  I
O  E  A  N  O  A  E  S  U  A  P  O  N  E  M
R  R  B  R  G  L  C  R  B  E  A  T  U  R  R
H  O  G  E  S  L  F  E  N  D  I  O  X  I  N
T  V  O  R  M  L  O  E  R  E  F  L  E  X  E
R  I  S  O  A  M  L  N  O  I  T  A  T  U  M
A  N  I  M  A  L  S  P  E  C  I  E  S  F  L
I  R  M  F  O  O  R  G  A  N  I  S  M  E  A
T  A  D  P  O  L  E  N  D  S  I  I  G  N  S
M  C  O  F  L  E  C  N  A  T  S  I  S  E  R
I  F  T  A  T  I  B  A  H  E  C  Y  C  L  E
```

AMOEBA
ANATOMY
ANIMAL SPECIES
ARTHROPODS
BACTERIA
CARNIVORE
CELL WALL
CYCLE
DIOXIN
FAMILY
FOSSIL
FUNGUS
GENETICS
GROWTH RINGS
HABITAT
KINSHIP
LUNGS
MAMMAL
MENOPAUSE
MUTATION
OMNIVORE
ORGANISM
OSMOSIS
POLLEN
REFLEX
RESISTANCE
RETINA
TADPOLE
TISSUE

UNCANNY TURN

Rearrange the letters of the words below to form a new word or phrase that is related to it in some way. The answer can be one or more words.

PRANCED RANTING

_____

★★★ BrainSnack®—Odd Number

Which of the numbers shown below is the odd one out?

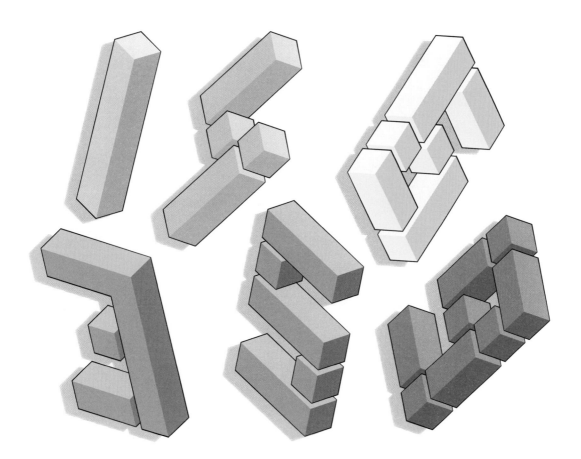

DOODLE PUZZLE

A doodle puzzle is a combination of images, letters and/or numbers that represent a word or a concept. If you cannot solve a doodle puzzle, do not look at the answer right away. Think hard—and outside the box.

★★ Teaser

ACROSS

- **1** Goblet
- **5** Elucidate
- **9** Prophecies
- **10** Truncheon
- **11** Heavy antelope
- **12** Chill
- **13** Musical
- **15** Man/goat deity
- **17** Banded chalcedony
- **20** Secreted
- **21** Enervate
- **23** Fencing action
- **27** Imperative
- **30** Chews
- **32** Munitions depot
- **33** Intimidated
- **34** Metropolitan
- **35** Circular
- **36** Abominates
- **37** Bitterness

DOWN

- **1** Brass percussion instrument
- **2** Cyberspace persona
- **3** Facetious
- **4** Exhilarating
- **5** Assemble
- **6** Appraise
- **7** Unbroken

©Lovatts Puzzles

- **8** Mast crossbeam end
- **14** World's largest democracy
- **16** Incendiarism
- **17** Trouble
- **18** Bristly grass tip
- **19** Brink
- **22** Unhoused
- **24** Deposes
- **25** More merciful
- **26** Into pieces
- **28** Hinder
- **29** Serving utensils
- **30** Wheat protein
- **31** Melanin-deficient creature

★ Cage the Animals

Draw the lines that will completely divide up the grid into smaller squares, representing cages, with exactly one animal per cage. Each cage can be as small as a single grid square. The cages cannot overlap.

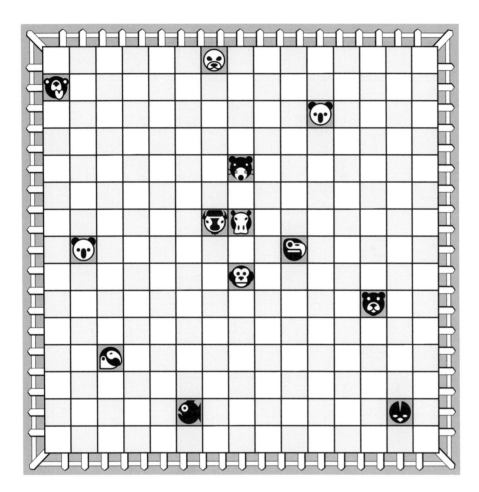

CHANGE ONE

Change one letter in each of these two words to form a common two-word phrase.

TEA CHARGE

_____   _____

★★★ Binairo

Complete the grid with zeros and ones until there are six zeros (0) and six ones (1) in every row and every column. No more than two of the same number can be next to or under each other. Rows or columns with exactly the same content are not allowed. There is only one valid solution per puzzle.

	0										
									0		
	1		1								
		0		0		1	1				
1	0										
					0	0				1	
	1									1	
		1		0	0				1		
									1	1	
			1		1	1				1	
	1		0					0			
				0		1		0	0		

DOODLE PUZZLE

A doodle puzzle is a combination of images, letters and/or numbers that represent a word or a concept. If you cannot solve a doodle puzzle, do not look at the answer right away. Think hard—and outside the box.

★★ Teaser

ACROSS

1 Orderly
6 Raise (eyebrows)
10 Reluctant
11 Beach wading bird
12 Brown sugar type
14 Gaped at
16 Attentive
18 Fragment
20 Expressing point of view
22 More severe
23 Secreted amount
25 Flagrancy
28 Tropical American epiphyte
29 Giraffe relative
31 Amend
32 Alienating

DOWN

1 Spy
2 Samovar drink
3 Earth colour
4 Fix in place
5 Non-perennials
7 Stave off
8 Genetically transmitted
9 Antithesis
13 Boredom
15 Inconceivable
17 Startle
19 Alarm
21 Nasty sprites
22 Slur
24 Rich garlic dressing
26 Bedeck
27 Projecting part of building
30 French friend

©Lovatts Puzzles

★★ Keep Going

Starting on a blank square of your choice, connect as many blank squares as possible with one single continuous line. You can only connect squares along vertical and horizontal lines, not along diagonal lines. You must continue the connecting line up until the next obstacle, i.e. the rim of the box, a black square or a square that has already been used. You can change direction at any obstacle you meet. Each square can only be used once. The number of blank squares that will be left unused is marked in the upper square. There is more than one solution. We only show one solution.

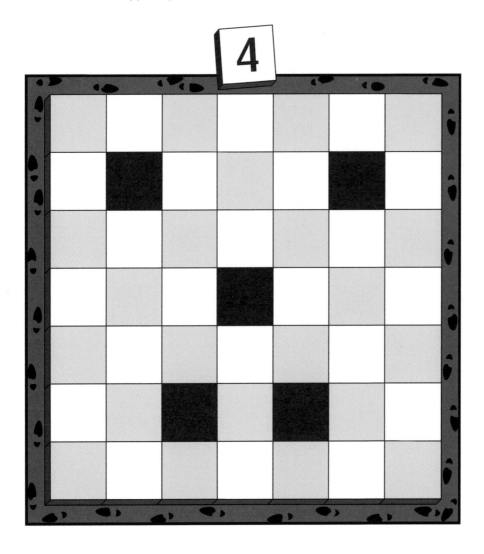

FRIENDS

What same word or affix can be added to the following to make new words?

AIR AMID APPRENTICE CITIZEN COURT
FRIEND MUSICIAN

★ Word Sudoku

Complete the grid so that each row, each column and each 3 x 3 frame contains the nine letters from the black box below. A nine-letter word is hidden in the diagonal from top left to bottom right.

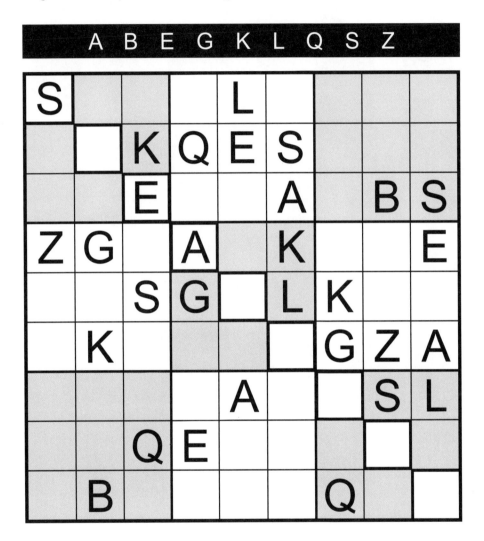

A B E G K L Q S Z

SANDWICH

What five-letter word belongs between the word at left and the word at right, so that the first and second word, and the second and third word, each form a common compound word?

NEWS _ _ _ _ _ CRAFT

★★★ Gourmet

ACROSS

1 Scottish rolls
4 Pelinkovac flavouring
8 Tinned fish
9 Italian tomato variety
10 Popular doughnut topping
11 Custard apple
13 Leaf vegetable
15 Surround by
17 Rye bread, eg
19 Modify
21 French, or ___, beans
23 Archetypical British pasty
26 Treat meat to make it softer
29 Thin Italian breadsticks
30 Potentially toxic Japanese food
31 Rigatoni or penne, eg
32 Rational
33 Legume seed

©Auspac Media

DOWN

1 Beet soup
2 Olive stuffing
3 Vietnamese dipping sauce (4,3)
4 Eccentric
5 Whisky, vermouth and bitters cocktail
6 Gilt bronze
7 Cooked
12 Source of agar
14 250 ml
15 Italian first courses
16 Should
18 Native meat, informal
20 Factor that affects boiling temperatures
22 Braised French beef stew (2,5)
24 Province
25 Bird chilli
27 Crème de la crème
28 Food that can be shirred

★★★ Sport Maze

Draw the shortest route from the golf ball to the hole. You can only move along vertical and horizontal lines, not along diagonal lines. The figure in each square indicates the number of squares the ball must be moved in the same direction. You can change directions at each stop. You can also retrace your path. The hole must be entered with the exact number of moves shown on the last square.

2	1	5	1	4	1
3	1	4	1	3	1
1	1	1	0	1	1
5	2	3	3	2	4
5	4	4	4	3	5
	5	4	3	1	0

LETTERBLOCKS

Move the letter blocks around to form two words, one on the top line, the other on the bottom line, that can be associated with exercise. Letters can be moved from one line to the other.

F	C	E	O	T	I	B
A	S	I	N	R	S	E

_ _ _ _ _ _ _

_ _ _ _ _ _ _

★★ Sudoku X

Fill in the grid so that each row, each column and each 3 x 3 frame contains every number from 1 to 9. The two main diagonals of the grid also contain every number from 1 to 9.

9	5	4	8	7	6		3	
	1					6	4	7
2							5	
7				2				8
5	8	6	9	3		4		
		3	7				6	
					7	5		6
					4			
			8					

REPOSITION PREPOSITION

Unscramble the words below and find a three-word phrase.

TIP IF NOON

_____ _____ _____

★★★ Tricky Teaser

ACROSS

1 Lemon-like fruit
7 Relieve
10 Informative
11 Happy
12 Wound with knife
13 Tinted
15 Medieval guitar
17 Dove call
18 Male sheep
20 Scarlet
21 Money fold
23 Scrape (out a living)
24 Born as
26 Fling
27 Resource
29 Verge
31 Journey
32 Excursion
33 Gown
35 Ledger entry
37 Notion
39 Sphere
41 Deceive
42 Golf peg
43 Border
44 Label
45 Outflow
47 Musical group
50 Support
52 Equipment
53 Slippery fish
54 Small improvements
55 Cleaning agent, caustic ___
56 Daze

© Lovatts Puzzles

DOWN

1 Reasoning
2 Pastures
3 Swirl
4 Corrosive fluid
5 Flashes (of lightning)
6 Duck or chicken
7 Orient
8 Modified
9 Implant
14 Stop
16 Grecian pot
18 Admire
19 Encountering
22 Daisy-like flower
25 Spooky
26 Coal by-product
27 Charitable funding
28 Add (up)
30 Age
34 Attack vigorously
36 Climbed on (plane)
38 Most penetrating
40 Receptacle
42 Foot digit
43 Angry outbursts
46 Prairie animal
48 Region
49 Droplet
50 Pay attention to
51 Allows to

★★★ BrainSnack®—Star Tripper

The space probe has already visited four star systems (not numbered) in a certain order. In which order will it visit the other systems, numbered 1 to 4? Answer like this: 2143.

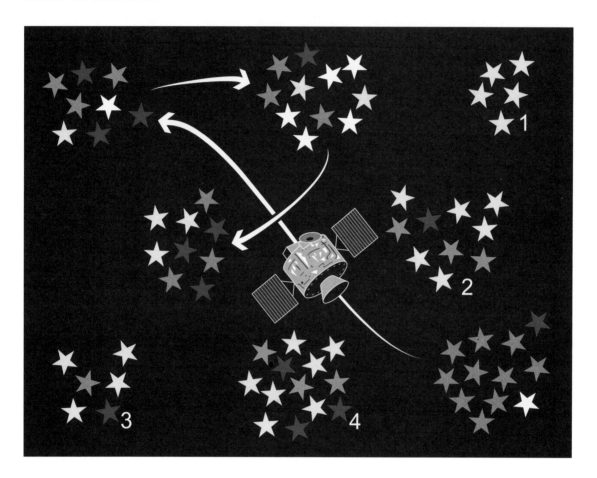

DOUBLETALK

What four-letter word means 'a breeze' or 'to tighten a spring'?

— — — —

★ Word Pyramid

Each word in the pyramid has the letters of the word above it, plus a new letter.

M
(1) I
(2) large Australian bird
(3) donkey
(4) feather
(5) wharf labourer
(6) collapse or fold
(7) thin device to pluck a guitar string

TRANSADDITION

Add one letter to letters from the words below and rearrange the rest to find a word that is related to the original phrase.

CUMIN DANCE

_____

★★ Bring Me Sunshine

The arrows below point in the direction of spots where the sun will shine, shown by the sun symbol. One spot is already shown. Can you locate the other spots? The sun symbols cannot adjoin each other vertically, horizontally or diagonally. A symbol cannot be placed on top of an arrow.

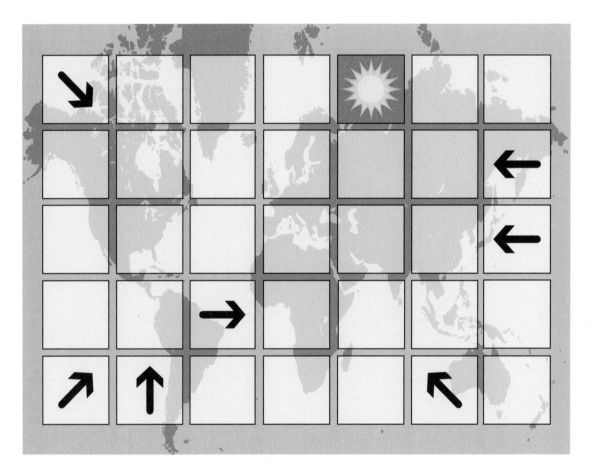

TAKE THE HINT

Use the letters from the words given in capitals to form the word that is described in the brackets. Write your answer in the row of letter blocks. Two additional letters are already in place.

TEA DRESS (hostess)

S			W					

★★★ On the Road

ACROSS

1 One who deals in cars, for instance
4 Becomes completely blocked (6,2)
10 Type of 911 Porsche
11 Engine-powered vehicle
12 Move past another vehicle travelling in the same direction
13 Modifies
14 Takes a seat
15 Maintenance that may delay drivers of vehicles
18 Travelling about (2,3,4)
20 Short trip in a motor car
23 Extremely sad or distressing
24 Long-term plan
27 Fastest land animal
28 Old type of car, especially one built between 1919 and 1930
29 Thoroughfare that takes traffic around the edge of a city (4,4)
30 Worn away or tattered along the edges

DOWN

1 Gauge that monitors engine revs

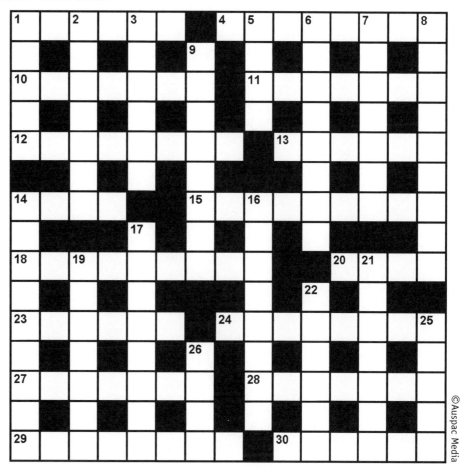

© Auspac Media

2 Channel, tube, or pipe which forms part of a ventilation system (3,4)
3 Throws out
5 Habitual dwelling place, usually where one's car is garaged
6 Method of changing gear in a car with automatic gear transmission
7 Captain of a team
8 Continues, often in spite of difficulties or opposition (7,2)
9 Holden 4WD model
14 Vehicle designed for speed, high acceleration, and manoeuvrability (6,3)
16 Substance put into petrol, for example, to improve its performance
17 Device that clears a car windscreen of condensation
19 Used car given in part payment of a new car (5-2)
21 Mini-MPV made by Mazda
22 Placard or sign carried in a procession or demonstration
25 Give way under pressure
26 The upmarket version of Ford's Fairmont

★ Sudoku Twin

Fill in the grid so that each row, each column and each 3 x 3 frame contains every number from 1 to 9. A sudoku twin is two connected 9 x 9 sudokus.

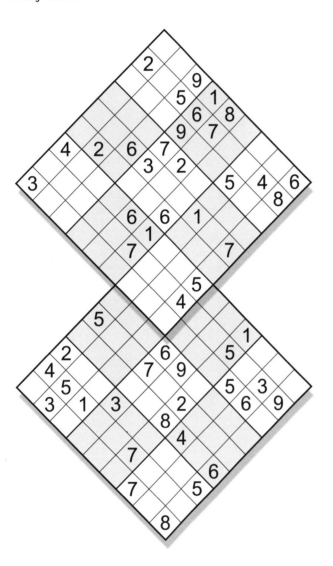

MISSING LETTER PROVERB

Fill in each missing letter, indicated by an X, to make a well-known proverb.

XAMXLIXRXTY XREXDX XONTXMPT

★ Cage the Animals

Draw the lines that will completely divide up the grid into smaller squares, representing cages, with exactly one animal per cage. Each cage can be as small as a single grid square. The cages cannot overlap.

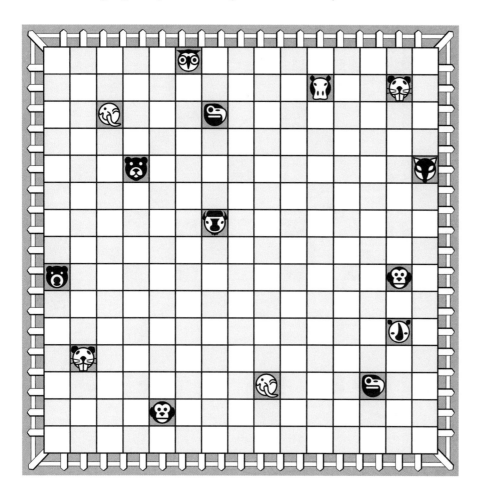

END GAME

The words you are seeking all have the letters END in them in the position indicated. When you have found all of the answers, from the clues on the right, one column will reveal the END GAME word which is not so easy.

_ _ _ _ E N D _	A Spanish house or estate
_ _ _ E N D _ _	Additional material
_ _ _ _ _ E N D	A clergyman
_ _ _ E N D _ _	Relied

★★★ Tricky Teaser

ACROSS

1 Written test
7 Surprise attack
10 Comradeship
11 Treaty
12 Without charge
13 Use book
15 Towards interior of
17 The U of IOU
18 Male offspring
20 Sleeping couch
21 Wheat tip
23 Before (poetic)
24 Island flower wreath
26 Expel
27 Gauges worth of
29 Wound mark
31 Implement
32 Grows faint
33 New Zealand bird
35 Finger or toe
37 Competent
39 Expert
41 Oui's opposite
42 View
43 Attach
44 Silence
45 Lens cover
47 Percussion instrument
50 Jot
52 Unit of weight
53 Regulation
54 Sudden crises
55 Smoke tendril
56 Eager

DOWN

1 Not full
2 Gathers (interest)
3 Breed (with)
4 Domestic servant
5 Fellow-feeling
6 Match before final
7 Breach
8 Type of exercise
9 Fear greatly
14 What we breathe
16 No score
18 Making airtight
19 Having (to)
22 Room beneath a roof
25 Composition
26 Sturdy tree
27 Fishing pole
28 Pose (for artist)
30 Lament
34 Walks like duck
36 Beards
38 Since
40 Ostrich relative
42 Self-regard
43 Crooked
46 Groom feathers
48 Frolic
49 Red Planet
50 Ancient Peruvian
51 Arduous hike

©Lovatts Puzzles

★★★ BrainSnack®—Fingerprints

Which of the pieces, numbered 1 to 6, should replace the question mark?

DOODLE PUZZLE

A doodle puzzle is a combination of images, letters and/or numbers that represent a word or a concept. If you cannot solve a doodle puzzle, do not look at the answer right away. Think hard—and outside the box.

OTHER 1

★ The Spy Who Came in From the Cold

The puzzled librarian was so busy fixing THE GOOD READS notice board that she didn't see the stranger hovering beside the old card index files. The stranger pulled up a chair in front of them and took a piece of microfilm from his pocket and peered at it, holding it up to the light, then started to re-arrange the labels on the card index drawers according to these numbers, which were on the microfilm: 13, 16, 24, 17, 19, 15, 7, 3, 29, 8, 23, 20, 14, 30, 28, 12, 21, 9, 26, 11, 5, 10, 18, 25, 22, 6.
Can you decode the message?

LETTER LINE

Each word below—paired with a set of numbers—is a clue to another word. This word will have the same number of letters as digits in its paired number. When you have found that word, match up each letter with its paired digit—the digit will tell you which square below in which to place the letter. When all the letters are in the correct squares, they will make a word that means 'disclosure.'

1 2 5 6 7 8 3 4 RELEVANT; 2 5 2 3 6 7 9 1 LIFT;
1 8 9 7 DISTURBANCE; 1 2 7 6 8 10 KEEP.

1	2	3	4	5	6	7	8	9	10

★★★ The Gardener

ACROSS

3 Soil with pH less than 7

5 Fungal reproductive cell

8 Lady Palm genus

10 Restharrow genus

11 Bugbane cultivar (5,5)

13 St John's Wort genus

17 Narrow country road

20 Wet muddy ground

21 Water jug

22 Egyptian peninsula

23 Maple genus

24 Apple seed, eg

25 American autumn

27 Irish garden estate that has The Jealous Wall

31 Place with an emergent layer

34 Relating to leaves

35 Peppery root crop

36 *Mangifera indica*

37 Leg joint

© Auspac Media

DOWN

1 All of a plant's above-ground parts

2 Taxonomic group above genus

3 As quickly as you can (abbr.) (1,1,1,1)

4 Corn Lily genus

6 Make known widely

7 Dried grape

9 Plant from *Aquilegia* genus

12 Abbreviation of *Epidendrum* orchid genus

14 Snap bean cultivar (6,4)

15 Fruit from genus *Rubus*

16 Aqueduct

18 Cobs

19 Needle, eg

26 Custard Apple genus

28 Transport vehicle

29 Deer Grass genus

30 What poison ivy makes you

32 Deficiency in lime-induced chlorosis

33 Serotiny is seed release in response to ____

★★ Keep Going

Starting on a blank square of your choice, connect as many blank squares as possible with one single continuous line. You can only connect squares along vertical and horizontal lines, not along diagonal lines. You must continue the connecting line up until the next obstacle, i.e. the rim of the box, a black square or a square that has already been used. You can change direction at any obstacle you meet. Each square can only be used once. The number of blank squares that will be left unused is marked in the upper square. There is more than one solution. We only show one solution.

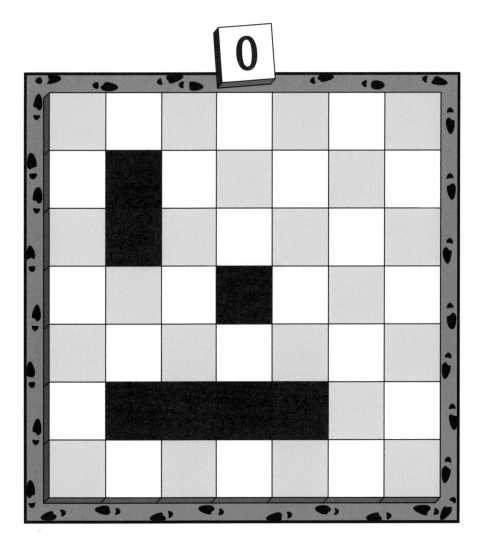

DELETE ONE

Delete one letter from ON PAST INCOMES and rearrange the rest to find a basis for reimbursement.

★ Athletics

All the words are hidden vertically, horizontally or diagonally—in both
directions. The letters that remain unused form a sentence from left to right.

```
U L T R A M A R A T H O N Y A
T H E L E T S T A N D S I R C
D S R C T R A I N I N G S U I
I H S O A A S P O R T T H J A
S O S T O R W A S O R I G N I
C E N T D D Y P M U J H G I H
U S A N O I T A R A P E R P L
S L D Y P P C U L L M I A O S
T P N E I L W N O E A N V S Y
H O I L N I I A N K R D E E N
R D W K G L K E T D A O L L O
O I L T E C O J T C T O H D L
W U I V A S B M O E H R G R H
I M A R C O I R S H O T P U T
N J T O E L E R O I N U J H A
G E A B E K C L A S W S S I C
C C K O L Y M P I C G E O A E
H A M E S G E V A E R T L N D
```

BOEBKA
COACH
DECATHLON
DISCUS-THROWING
DOPING
GEVAERT
GRAVEL
HIGH JUMP
HURDLES
INDOOR
INJURY
JAVELIN
JOHNSON
JUNIOR
LEWIS
MARATHON
MILE
OUTDOOR
PODIUM
PREPARATION
RELAY RACE
SHOES
SHOT PUT
SPIKES
STANDS
STOPWATCH
TAIL WIND
TRACK
TRAINING
ULTRAMARATHON

ONE LETTER LESS OR MORE

The word on the right side contains the letters of the word on the left side plus the letter in the
middle. What is the word? One letter is already in the right place.

| C | H | A | R | I | S | M | A | +R | | R | | | | | | |

★★★ Tricky Teaser

ACROSS

1 Dull
7 Uncured bacon
10 Unreasonably
11 Steel strand
12 Catch sight of
13 Trade
15 The one there
17 Glide on snow
18 Tell untruth
20 Large deer
21 Purring animal
23 Commotion
24 Battle
26 Chinese pans
27 Indexes
29 Soviet states
    (1,1,1,1)
31 Bucket
32 Period of time
33 Indian dress
35 Cut into cubes
37 Pimple rash
39 Section of play
41 And not
42 Wool thickness
43 Vat
44 Helium or
    hydrogen
45 Young lion
47 Forbids
50 Bouncing toy
52 Lash
53 Exude
54 Conclusion
55 Minus
56 Camp shelter

©Lovatts Puzzles

DOWN

1 Arrives (of day)
2 Nauseous in flight
3 Puffed
4 Circuit
5 Fluids
6 Mode of walking
7 Fervent request
8 Pearl-bearers
9 Paddling craft
14 Well-suited

16 Chop with axe
18 Shortcoming
19 Worries
22 Meat jelly
25 Of the ear
26 Used to be
27 Top
28 Lump of turf
30 Fish eggs
34 Hare relatives
36 Persuading

38 Violent tropical
    storm
40 Metal can
42 Pod vegetable
43 Absorbent cloth
46 Lamb's cry
48 Gorillas or
    orang-utans
49 Any
50 Nibble
51 Plunder

★★★ Sport Maze

Draw the shortest route from the golf ball to the hole. You can only move along vertical and horizontal lines, not along diagonal lines. The figure in each square indicates the number of squares the ball must be moved in the same direction. You can change directions at each stop. You can also retrace your path. The hole must be entered with the exact number of moves shown on the last square.

4	5	1	5	5	2
1	4	4	1	2	5
2	1	2	3	4	4
3	4	2		0	3
5	4	4	3	1	5
3	1	3	1	3	1

UNCANNY TURN

Rearrange the letters of the words below to form a new word or phrase that is related to it in some way. The answer can be one or more words.

NINE THUMPS

_____

★★★ The Gourmet

ACROSS

1 Kitchen helper
5 Cicely, eg
9 Vegetable or fruit condiment
11 Edible French snails
13 Asian sugar
14 Italian 5 Across
16 Jaggery
17 Scandinavian spirit
18 French poaching broth
21 Dry, of wine
23 Metallic food wrapping
24 Black food colouring, squid ___
26 Common lettuce variety
28 Stay in a tent
30 Flavour extracts
31 Melt down fat
32 Reflection
33 Moist Thai spice blend (5,5)

DOWN

1 Firm-fleshed fish, Silver or John ___
2 Whipped cream and wine dessert
3 Good wood for smoking food
4 German ice wine
6 Hot creamy alcoholic drink
7 Acidic dairy product
8 Russian yeast cake
10 Russian tea urn
12 Fortified wine
15 Cut shorter and thicker than julienne
19 Rich chocolate and cream mixture
20 Greek stuffed vegetables or grape leaves
22 Food show, 'Surfing ___ ___' (3,4)
23 Ancient Roman garment
25 Cherry brandy
27 Tallest active European volcano
29 Soft French cheese
31 Sun beam

©Auspac Media

★ Spot the Differences

There are nine differences between these two images. Can you find them? Circle the differences on the image on the right.

CHANGE ONE

Change one letter in each of these two words to form a common two-word phrase.

SHOOTING CATCH

_____ _____

★★★ Sudoku

Fill in the grid so that each row, each column and each 3 x 3 frame contains every number from 1 to 9.

						1		
4							2	
							6	4
	1				2			
	2	8		7	4			
9	7	6		5				
		1		4	7			9
		9		8	5			1
				1		7		2

MAGIC SQUARE

In this square, each row, column or diagonal totals 34. There are many ways that sets of four squares can total 34—for example, 4-1-16-13, 4-15-9-6, etc. How many can you find?

4	15	14	1
9	6	7	12
5	10	11	8
16	3	2	13

★★★ Word Sudoku

Complete the grid so that each row, each column and each 3 x 3 frame contains the nine letters from the black box below. A nine-letter word is hidden in the diagonal from top left to bottom right.

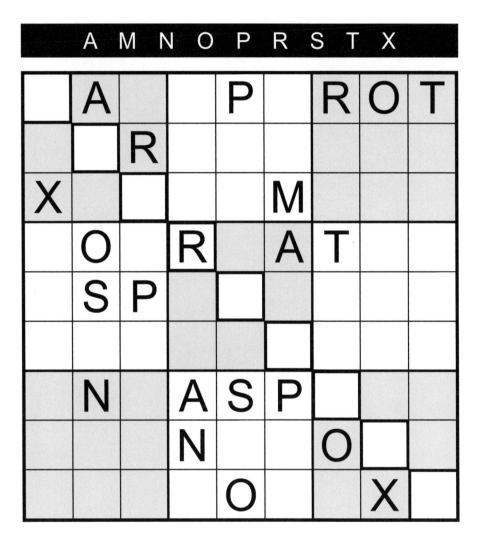

| A M N O P R S T X |

	A			P		R	O	T
		R						
X				M				
	O		R		A	T		
	S	P						
	N		A	S	P			
			N			O		
				O			X	

DOODLE PUZZLE

A doodle puzzle is a combination of images, letters and/or numbers that represent a word or a concept. If you cannot solve a doodle puzzle, do not look at the answer right away. Think hard—and outside the box.

★★★ BrainSnack®—Cubism

Which group of cubes, numbered from 1 to 5, is the odd one out?

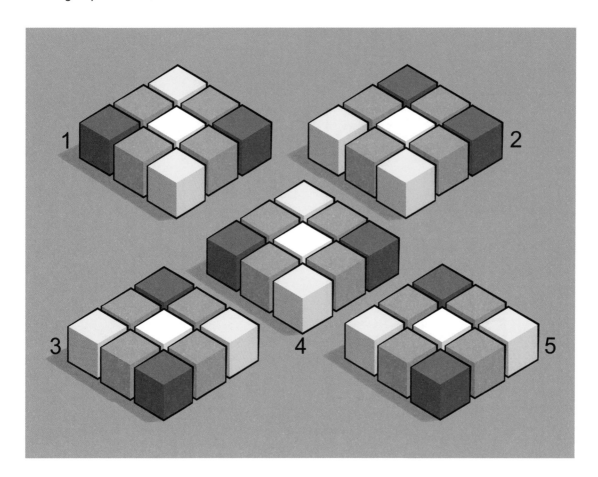

SUMMER SCHOOL

Fill the boxes with the numbers 1 to 9 to give the correct row, column and diagonal totals.

			17
	4		10
			18
15	16	14	19

★★ Circuit Breaker

How many words of 4 letters or more can you make from these 9 letters? In making a word each letter may be used only once, and the centre letter must be included. No slang, foreign words, hyphens, apostrophes, or plurals ending in 's'. Source: Collins Dictionary

TARGET
GOOD 23; VERY GOOD 29; EXCELLENT 35; GENIUS 41

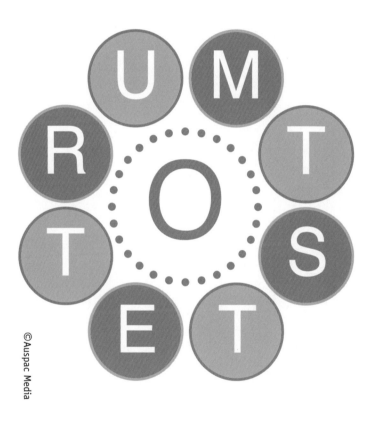

©Auspac Media

★ Cage the Animals

Draw the lines that will completely divide up the grid into smaller squares, representing cages, with exactly one animal per cage. Each cage can be as small as a single grid square. The cages cannot overlap.

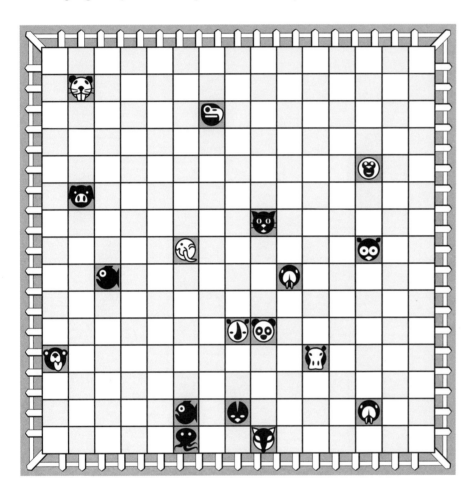

FRIENDS

What same word or affix can be added to the following to make new words?

BORE DUKE FREE KING OFFICIAL RAN STAR

★★ Binairo

Complete the grid with zeros and ones until there are five zeros (0) and six ones (1) in every row and every column. No more than two of the same number can be next to or under each other. Rows or columns with exactly the same content are not allowed. There is only one valid solution per puzzle.

I										
										I
			I							
			O						O	
		I		I	I		I	I		
										O
						O				O
		O		I		O		O		
O					O				I	
	O	O				O			I	I

SANDWICH

What four-letter word belongs between the word at left and the word at right, so that the first and second word, and the second and third word, each form a common compound word or phrase?

THUMB __ __ __ __ BRUSH

★★★ Tricky Teaser

ACROSS

1 Professions
7 Enthusiastic review
10 Sped up
11 Carbonated drink
12 Action word
13 Prayer ending
15 Shocked inhalation
17 Daylight provider
18 Flying mammal
20 Surface (road)
21 Snooker stick
23 Raw mineral
24 Electric fish
26 Retain
27 Lock of hair
29 Ancient harp
31 Settled (debt)
32 Dull crash
33 Likeable
35 Uncanny
37 Compass point
39 Large vase
41 Umpire
42 Ball
43 Young bear
44 Pig enclosure
45 Line (of seats)
47 Concept
50 Story
52 Step
53 Lessen
54 Tears
55 Antlered animal
56 Virile man

©Lovatts Puzzles

DOWN

1 Car hoists
2 Equilibrium
3 Confidence trick
4 Sighted
5 State
6 Vampire's tooth
7 Races (motor)
8 Proficiently
9 Glowing coal
14 Make last, ___ out
16 Wonder
18 Fringes
19 Give evidence
22 Top (section)
25 More senior
26 Relatives
27 Neck garment
28 Feminine pronoun
30 Dine
34 Shower stall
36 Flee from foes
38 Side-by-side
40 Formerly known as
42 Egg cells
43 Managed
46 Exercise (power)
48 Expensive
49 Region
50 Stumble
51 Camera glass

★ Astronomy

All the words listed are hidden vertically, horizontally or diagonally—in both directions. The letters that remain unused form a sentence from left to right.

```
G A L I L E O B I G B A N G A
J U P I T E R Z O D I A C S T
R O N O Y S P V N E P T U N E
M Y Y I R R S L E L B B U H O
M A R S U E Y S U N A R U E N
E W O F C V R S A T U R N L T
H Y P E R I O N H E O S F I E
A K O W E N T C O M E T L O S
W L L C M U A E I R E E E C T
K I A N C E V N S O I K V E E
I M R N W O R T H E I C A N L
N C I H L A E A R T H O R T E
G M S L A T S U E E U R T R S
P H O T O N B R R M S C E I C
A P N P L A O X Y G E N C S O
A N D R O M E D A N A S A M P
Y T I V A R G Y A N A C P T E
I V E R E A L U B E N O S L E
```

ANDROMEDA
APOLLO
BIG BANG
CENTAUR
COMET
EARTH
GALILEO
GRAVITY
HAWKING
HELIOCENTRISM
HUBBLE
HYPERION
JUPITER
MARS
MERCURY
METEOR
MILKY WAY
NASA
NEBULAE
NEPTUNE
OBSERVATORY
OXYGEN
PHOTON
PLUTO
POLARIS
ROCKET
SATURN
SPACE TRAVEL
TELESCOPE
UNIVERSE
URANUS
VENUS
ZODIAC

LETTERBLOCKS

Move the letter blocks around to form two words, one on the top line, the other on the bottom line, that can be associated with countries. Letters can be moved from one line to the other.

G N D E L A N

R N Y G M A E

_ _ _ _ _ _ _

_ _ _ _ _ _ _

★★ Keep Going

Starting on a blank square of your choice, connect as many blank squares as possible with one single continuous line. You can only connect squares along vertical and horizontal lines, not along diagonal lines. You must continue the connecting line up until the next obstacle, i.e. the rim of the box, a black square or a square that has already been used. You can change direction at any obstacle you meet. Each square can only be used once. The number of blank squares that will be left unused is marked in the upper square. There is more than one solution. We only show one solution.

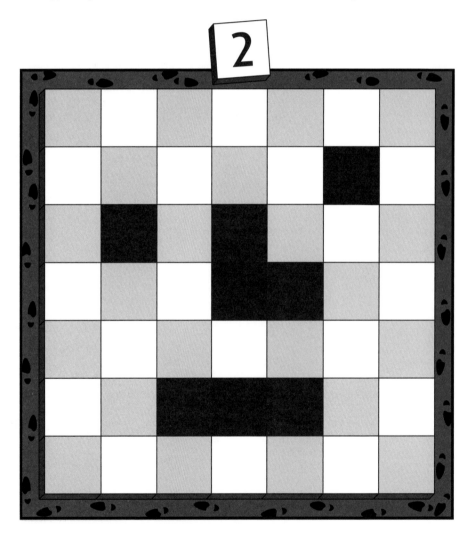

REPOSITION PREPOSITION

Unscramble TITAN DOWN THINGS and find a one-word preposition.

★★★ On the Road

ACROSS

1 Something, like a concept car, made for a special occasion (3-3)

5 Power-packed car built by Chrysler Australia in the 1970s

10 Have a go; negotiate a corner (4,1,4)

11 Heavy dull sounds

12 Supermodel

13 Substance used in a radiator, especially in cold regions

15 Large motor car, with ample room for passengers and luggage

16 Small car, esp. one for use in a town

19 There won't be much of this in a small car containing tall people

20 Turned a car completely over

23 Putting on a seatbelt (8,2)

25 Part of a brake that comes in contact with a wheel

27 Main line in the arterial network

28 Means of protecting or safeguarding against risk or injury

©Auspac Media

29 Device that allows 4WDs to take in air especially when making water crossings

30 Material that tyres are made out of

DOWN

2 Austrian motor-racing driver, born 1949 (4,5)

3 Green light

4 Easy and graceful in motion

5 Go forward

6 Electrical machine that generates a current in vehicles

7 Sort of device that shows how much is left in 14 Down, for example

8 Treat with consideration

9 Public road

14 Fuel container (6,4)

17 Something normally done during a regular service (3,6)

18 Competitive ski event

19 Metal coverings fitted to the centre of wheels

21 Fuel used by most trucks

22 Popular type of Nissan car

24 Goods carried by a large vehicle

26 Dull and monotonous

★★★ Sport Maze

Draw the shortest route from the golf ball to the hole. You can only move along vertical and horizontal lines, not along diagonal lines. The figure in each square indicates the number of squares the ball must be moved in the same direction. You can change directions at each stop. You can also retrace your path. The hole must be entered with the exact number of moves shown on the last square.

	5	5	5	2	1 (hole)
2	3	1	4	2	1
3	3	0	3	3	2
4	2	3	2	2	5
4	2	4	1	2	1
1	2	1	2	1	2

DOUBLETALK

What five-letter word means 'to adhere' or 'a piece of wood'?

_ _ _ _ _

★★★ Kakuro

Each number in a black square is the sum of the numbers to be filled in the adjacent empty boxes. The empty boxes that make up the sum are called a run. The sum of the 'across run' is written above the diagonal in the black area, and the sum of the 'down run' is written below the diagonal. Runs can contain only the numbers 1 to 9 and each number in a run can be used only once. The grey boxes contain only odd numbers and the white only even numbers.

TRANSADDITION

Add one letter to letters from the words below and rearrange the rest to find a word that is related to the original phrase.

LENT RACE ID

★★★ Tricky Teaser

ACROSS

1 String tangle
7 Uterus
10 Preventative injection
11 School test
12 Air duct
13 Sport squad
15 Ale
17 Hawaiian garland
18 Not high
20 Be in arrears
21 Ancient
23 Historical period
24 Flightless bird
26 Of sound mind
27 Wizards' rods
29 Tiny landmass
31 Competed
32 Dress-up toy
33 Nobleman
35 Commence
37 Variety
39 Modern
41 Flee
42 Exercise club
43 Cyclone centre
44 Slump
45 Unruly crowd
47 Matured
50 Certain
52 Unzip
53 Banded quartz
54 Appointments
55 Ocean phase
56 Transmit

© Lovatts Puzzles

DOWN

1 Rest on knees
2 Great applause
3 Bring under control
4 Floating filth
5 Mythical horned horse
6 Strike (toe)
7 Interlaced
8 Very demanding
9 Cleanse (wound)
14 Tot up
16 Ram's mate
18 Frontrunners
19 Padding
22 Floodbank
25 White (of liquid)
26 Mournful
27 Spider's trap
28 Male offspring
30 Conclude
34 Worked (dough)
36 Stood sentry duty at
38 Gigantic
40 Misery
42 Wildebeest
43 Explode (of volcano)
46 Sparred
48 Departed
49 Pull
50 Plant stalk
51 Decays

★★★ BrainSnack®—Painter

Which of the paints, numbered from 1 to 4, was used the most to colour in the three shapes?

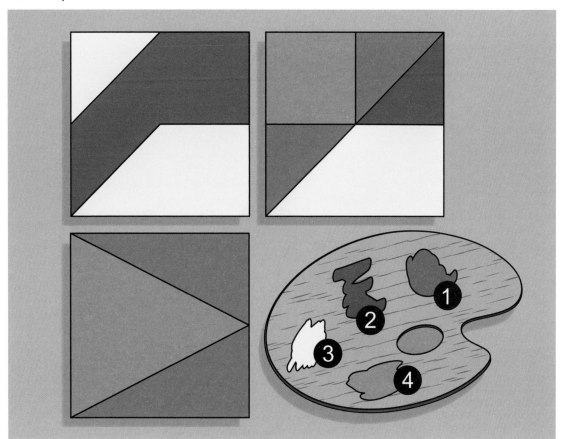

TAKE THE HINT

Use the letters from the words given in capitals to form the words that are described in the brackets. Write your answer in the row of letter blocks. One additional letter is already in the right place.

NORDIC ALP (major part of the central nervous system)

| S | | | | | | | | | | |

★★★ Word Sudoku

Complete the grid so that each row, each column and each 3 x 3 frame contains the nine letters from the black box below. A nine-letter word is hidden in the diagonal from top left to bottom right.

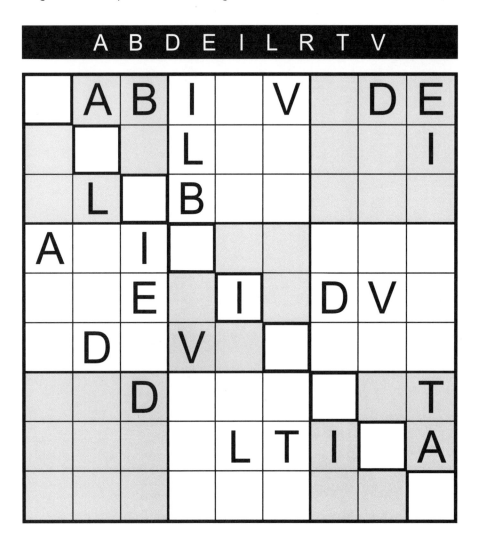

MISSING LETTER PROVERB

Fill in each missing letter, indicated by an X, to make a well-known proverb.

XILENXE IX XOLXEN

★★★ BrainSnack®—Number Block

What number should replace the question mark?

END GAME

The words you are seeking all have the letters END in them in the position indicated. When you have found all of the answers, from the clues on the right, one column will reveal the END GAME word which radiates.

			E	N	D			Riser
_	_	_	E	N	D	_	_	Straightened
		_	E	N	D	_	_	Repaired again
_	_	E	N	D	_	_	_	Altering

★★★ The Gourmet

ACROSS

1 Indian spice, ___ caraway
4 Sweet pepper
9 Potato variety, ___ Burbank
10 Cogent
11 Egg option
14 Potato part
15 Creamy curry that includes yogurt
16 Middle Eastern yogurt cheese
18 Main ingredient in braunschweiger
21 Japanese glutinous rice cake
22 Chook's bed
23 Had a meal
26 And so on (abbr.)
27 Mexican bean preparation
30 Bread platter
32 Monotony
33 Clear mixer
34 Famous Chinese duck dish

© Auspac Media

DOWN

1 Southeast Asian liquor, made from coconut flowers
2 Chinese sauce
3 Japanese fermented soybeans
5 Make someone feel embarrassed
6 Glide over snow
7 Whole fruit jam
8 Flavour of sharaab ettoot
11 'Palm tree' pastry
12 Fossilised resin
13 Watered down
17 Garlic mayonnaise
19 Swiss cheese
20 Dondurma, eg (3,5)
24 Sesame seed paste
25 Sister spice to mace
28 Paddock
29 Tuck in! (3,2)
31 Tin

★★ Sudoku X

Fill in the grid so that each row, each column and each 3 x 3 frame contains every number from 1 to 9. The two main diagonals of the grid also contain every number from 1 to 9.

								2
					1	8		7
		8	4	2			3	1
7							5	8
			2		4	9		3
3		4		5	9			
8		1						
9			5	3			2	
				9	6	7		

UNCANNY TURN

Rearrange the letters of the words below to form a new word or phrase that is related to it in some way. The answer can be one or more words.

DEBIT CARD

★ Cage the Animals

Draw the lines that will completely divide up the grid into smaller squares, representing cages, with exactly one animal per cage. Each cage can be as small as a single grid square. The cages cannot overlap.

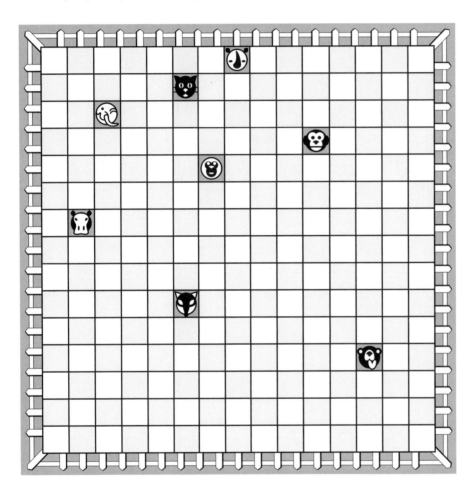

SUMMER SCHOOL

Fill the boxes with the numbers 1 to 9 to give the correct row, column and diagonal totals.

	4		15
			17
			13
17	11	17	22

★★★ On the Road

ACROSS

1 Maker of the Accent, Elantra and Sonata
5 Accessory required to transport around a small child (3,4)
9 Out of order
10 Trial conducted by a prospective buyer of a car (4,5)
11 Motor vehicle suffering badly from corrosion (4,6)
12 Type of car that's traded in
14 Irritating noise, the sort made by an unoiled door hinge
16 Small bar or restaurant
19 Maker of the Matiz, Lanos and Nubira
20 Heavy fuel oil
23 Spacious or uncluttered
24 Main revolving rod of an engine that transmits motion or power
27 One of Renault's Scenic range
28 Enthusiasm, vigour or energy
29 Something the panelbeaters may have to do to repair paintwork
30 A candidate for a 5 Across (4,3)

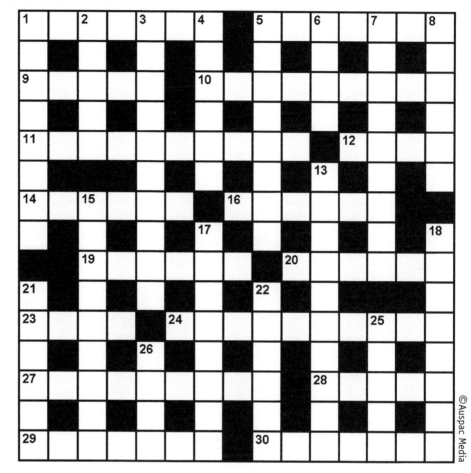

©Auspac Media

DOWN

1 Cushioned frame fitted to the top of a seat in a car
2 Single elements
3 They may be applied to slow down a vehicle (4,6)
4 Untouched
5 The sort of improvements made by detailers
6 Travel in a vehicle
7 Waste discharged by an engine, for example
8 Stylish
13 Removes parts from a car, for instance (6,4)
15 Supports from beneath
17 Kind of car supplied to temporarily replace a broken-down vehicle
18 At full speed (4,4)
21 Motorhome
22 Loose sheet placed within the folds of a newspaper or periodical
25 Let in
26 The support of an arch, bridge, etc

★★ Keep Going

Starting on a blank square of your choice, connect as many blank squares as possible with one single continuous line. You can only connect squares along vertical and horizontal lines, not along diagonal lines. You must continue the connecting line up until the next obstacle, i.e. the rim of the box, a black square or a square that has already been used. You can change direction at any obstacle you meet. Each square can only be used once. The number of blank squares that will be left unused is marked in the upper square. There is more than one solution. We only show one solution.

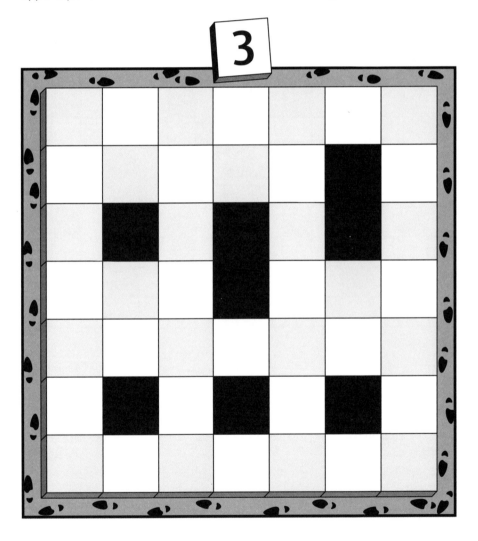

DELETE ONE

Delete one letter from FITS MANIACS and rearrange the rest to find a description of excessive dedication.

★ Telecommunications

All the words listed are hidden vertically, horizontally or diagonally—in both directions. The letters that remain unused form a sentence from left to right.

```
I N L A C O L C O M P A N Y T
M H E P A S T I F Y S O U W A
B E A M O F L I G H T O E N T
E W S D T I O P L L H X U E I
K I O S N E D A S L P O L N M
A R E M A C N A E E O B T N D
E E O D T G H E R B A E Y E S
N L Y W I O E I U C R P V T P
R E L S T G M S E N S I E A E
S S E A D E I A E B C L G N A
C S U X N T N T T E I O A T K
N I T T E O O A A B T A M E E
T C R R A L Z C O L T N I N R
T H H T E S E M A T T A E N N
F A X A C T E T I O N L O A F
T H I N T E R N A T I O N A L
C H A N N E L E D S W G I T C
H B O A R D O E P E R A T O R
```

ANALOG
ANTENNA
BEAM OF LIGHT
BELL
BYTE
CABLE
CAMERA
CHANNEL
CHAT
COMPANY
DEVICE
DIGITAL
ELECTRIC
EXPERIMENT
FAX
IMAGE
INTERNATIONAL
INTERNET
LOCAL
MESSAGES
MOBILE
NETWORK
RADIO
SEND
SIGNAL
SOUND
SPEAKER
TELEX
WIRELESS
ZONAL

CHANGE ONE

Change one letter in each of these two words to form a common two-word phrase.

BOLD SWEAR

_____

★★★ The Gardener

ACROSS

1 *Calliandra*, or Power ___ Plant
3 Hawaiian name for spurges
6 Young bovine
11 Wavy-toothed leaf margin
12 North American grassland
13 Large tank
14 Long narrow feedbox
15 Garden features often overcome with terraces
16 Public transport vehicle
18 Consumed
20 Australian wetland grass genus
22 Flower whose root is used in liqueurs and bitters
23 Big plant smaller than a tree
25 Concluding
28 Weeding tool
29 Destructive swarming insect
30 Dogwood genus
31 Leatherwork tool
33 Lettuce variety
34 Amaranth genus
35 Spinning toy (2-2)
36 Fleshy fruit with central stone
37 Inner bark fibre

©Auspac Media

DOWN

1 Flower variety with petals with different colour along the edges
2 Californian city in Alameda County
4 Home of the MM Gryshko National Botanical Garden
5 Held onto
7 Shrivel up
8 Fragrant flower, native to Africa
9 Suspended planter (7,6)
10 *Platycodon grandiflorus* (7,6)
16 Bouquet
17 Fern frond stalk
19 Liming agent for soils
21 Corn genus
23 Plant from *Tragopogon* genus
24 Alpine garden feature
26 Heavenly Bamboo genus
27 Most overgrown
31 Gelatinous substance from algae
32 Flaccid

★★★ BrainSnack®—Energy Saver

The owners of this modern house are trying to keep their energy use to a minimum. Each number stands for the use in a certain room. How much energy will be used in the room with the question mark (the main entrance)?

LETTER LINE

Each word below—paired with a set of numbers—is a clue to another word. This word will have the same number of letters as digits in its paired number. When you have found that word, match up each letter with its paired digit—the digit will tell you which square below in which to place the letter. When all the letters are in the correct squares, they will make a word that means 'inspiring fear.'

8 7 5 9 10 6 RELEASED ON BOND; 9 5 4 8 2 IN BETWEEN;
8 3 5 10 1 SHORT; 8 9 7 6 10 KNIFE; 8 10 6 9 7 4 CHAOS.

1	2	3	4	5	6	7	8	9	10

★★ Monkey Business

Some of the older students have been monkeying about with the BEST KIDS
BOOKS titles list in the library and have mixed up the letters of each title.
Can you unscramble each title to fix the list?

1 BEACHHEAD WIDOWER THROTTLE NINTH
by C.S. LEWIS

2 THAT TIN CHEETAH
by DR. SEUSS

3 DICK THE GULLY GUN
by HANS CHRISTIAN ANDERSEN

4 RATCHET ELBOWS
by E.B. WHITE

5 THE TWIST
by ROALD DAHL

ONE LETTER LESS OR MORE

The word on the right side contains the letters of the word on the left side plus the letter in the middle. What is the word? One letter is already in the right place.

LOCATION +I ☐ ☐ ☐ L ☐ ☐ ☐ ☐ ☐

★★★ The Gourmet

ACROSS

1 Cypriot cheese with high melting point
5 Braggart
10 Aussie vegetables
11 Grassland
12 Milk drunk by Bedouins
13 Picture recording device
15 Seafood and meat dish, ___ and turf
17 Devours
19 Asian pear
21 Thin biscuit served with ice cream
23 Italian apéritif
24 Smoothly crushed fruit
25 Swedish mulled wine
26 Fish whose roe are prized
29 Swindle
32 Long choux pastry
35 Frequently used part of a lemon
36 Korean pickles
37 Portable phone
38 British cheese and toast dish
39 Hot mustard

© Auspac Media

DOWN

2 Stadium
3 Popular cooking oil
4 Grape variety
6 Gin and lime cocktail
7 Unfreezes
8 Scrub clean
9 British berry and bread dessert (6,7)
13 Cocktail snacks
14 Tightwad
16 One who searches widely to find food
18 Chug
20 Decorates a cake
22 Plants of a region
27 Japanese brown seaweed
28 Chinese tea variety
30 Porcelain
31 French lamb's lettuce
33 Tin covering
34 Vegetates

★★★ Sport Maze

Draw the shortest way from the ball to the goal. You can only move along vertical and horizontal lines, not along diagonal lines. The figure on each square indicates the number of squares the ball must be moved in the same direction. You can change direction at each stop.

1	4	5	4	2	5
5	2	3	2	3	3
1	4	2	1	4	1
5	4	3	1	3	5
2	1	4	3	2	3
3	1	4	1	○	3

UNCANNY TURN

Rearrange the letters of the words below to form a new word or phrase that is related to it in some way. The answer can be one or more words.

MY MUM

★★★ Word Sudoku

Complete the grid so that each row, each column and each 3 x 3 frame contains the nine letters from the black box below. A nine-letter word is hidden in the diagonal from top left to bottom right.

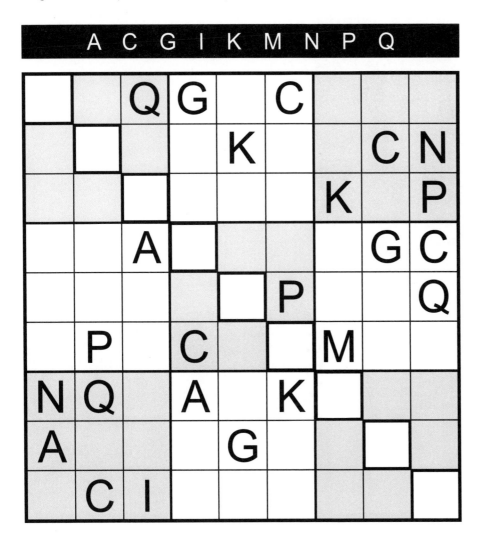

| A | C | G | I | K | M | N | P | Q |

		Q	G		C			
				K			C	N
					K		P	
		A					G	C
				P				Q
	P		C		M			
N	Q		A		K			
A				G				
	C	I						

DOODLE PUZZLE

A doodle puzzle is a combination of images, letters and/or numbers that represent a word or a concept. If you cannot solve a doodle puzzle, do not look at the answer right away. Think hard—and outside the box.

★ Spot the Differences

There are nine differences between these two images. Can you find them?
Circle the differences on the image on the right.

DELETE ONE

Delete one letter from CURE OR SPIN and rearrange the rest to find the dealers.

_____

★★★★ The Skeleton

The object is to complete the crossword even though we've removed the black squares. You'll find the design is fully symmetrical, not only top to bottom but also side to side. To start you off we've put in some numbers that should help you flesh out the grid with black squares. The Skeleton looks difficult but once you pick out the bones, you'll soon get the hang of it!

ACROSS

- **1** Coating with pan juices
- **6** Reconstructed
- **11** Carrion bird
- **12** Raise in rank
- **13** Great conductor
- **14** Frostily
- **16** Influenza
- **17** Dish up
- **19** That lady
- **20** Zero
- **21** Tuneful
- **23** Cruel people
- **25** Bequeathed
- **28** Admires
- **31** Ocean
- **32** Edge
- **33** Sceptic
- **35** Mire
- **36** Baby grand
- **37** Contaminate (environment)
- **39** Come to understand
- **41** Nags
- **42** Downward climb
- **43** Removes silt from

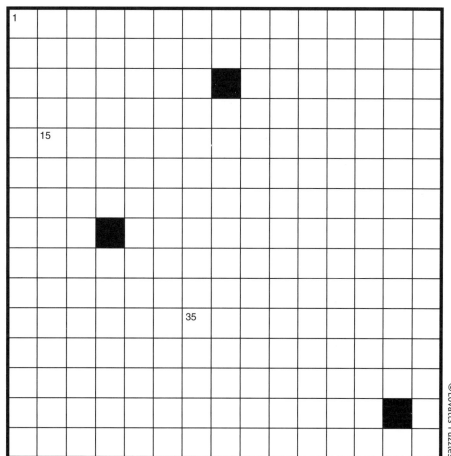

©Lovatts Puzzles

DOWN

- **1** Christening
- **2** Tales
- **3** Tusk material
- **4** Almond or cashew
- **5** Joyful
- **6** Hearsay reports
- **7** Historical age
- **8** Toots
- **9** Trainee doctors
- **10** Bricklaying tools
- **15** Fruit pickle
- **18** Thiamine or riboflavin
- **22** Dairy animal
- **24** Spot
- **25** Fled
- **26** Hangs
- **27** Faintest
- **28** Lasted
- **29** Wiping out
- **30** Cigarette users
- **34** Two-door car
- **36** Stage
- **38** Roman X
- **40** Go astray

★★ Sudoku X

Fill in the grid so that each row, each column and each 3 x 3 frame contains every number from 1 to 9. The two main diagonals of the grid also contain every number from 1 to 9.

2				8			
		4				5		
7								
		9	1					
8	3	6			2			
1			4					
	1				6	8		
	9	3		7			2	
	6				7		4	

FRIENDS

What same word or affix can be added to the following to make new words?

ACCIDENT CLERIC COMIC CRITIC LOGIC
NORM PERSON

★ Cage the Animals

Draw the lines that will completely divide up the grid into smaller squares, representing cages, with exactly one animal per cage. Each cage can be as small as a single grid square. The cages cannot overlap.

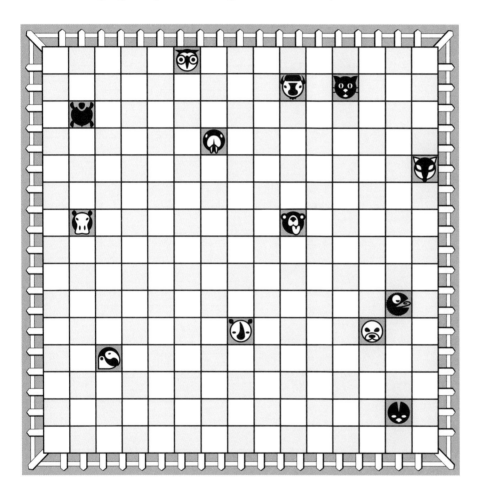

SANDWICH

What four-letter word belongs between the word at left and the word at right, so that the first and second word, and the second and third word, each form a common compound word ?

C O P P E R __ __ __ __ H U N T E R

★★ Circuit Breaker

How many words of 4 letters or more can you make from these 9 letters? In making a word each letter may be used only once, and the centre letter must be included. No slang, foreign words, hyphens, apostrophes, or plurals ending in 's'.
Source: Collins Dictionary

TARGET
GOOD 22; VERY GOOD 27; EXCELLENT 32; GENIUS 37

©Auspac Media

★★★ BrainSnack®—Parking Space

All but one of these cars, numbered from 1 to 11, have followed a particular pattern when parking. Which car is the odd one out?

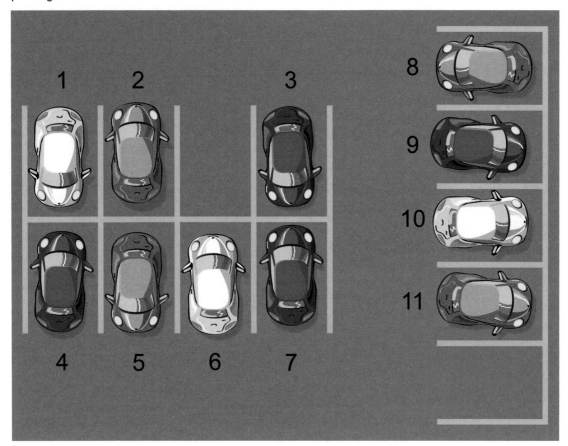

LETTERBLOCKS

Move the letter blocks around to form two words, one on the top line, the other on the bottom line, that can be associated with insects. Letters can be moved from one line to the other.

R * S E I D R _ _ _ _ _ _ _

E T C K I C P _ _ _ _ _ _ _

★ Agriculture

All the words listed are hidden vertically, horizontally or diagonally—in both directions. The letters that remain unused form a sentence from left to right.

```
C A G A S P A R A G U S R I C
A U L M T U E R E P R O D U C
R E S A F B O O E L T T A C D
R I A N M T I U R F F S W E L
O L R U A S W O R C E R A C S
T O C R B R E E D I N G N T H
E U R E I G L H O O N W N D S
C S C S U G B C O H E O U L A
V S A U M F A C L R L D A I O
E W U R O E T T H R S A L A P
G B L P O S S Y I I S E F L I
E A I L R W T C R O C M A F N
T R F U H O F O Y E N O I U S
A L L S S C T R M T L L R D R
B E O E U A T C H A H E E Y A
L Y W E M R A N A D T E C B P
E S E M U G E L I R W O O F U
E Y R T L U O P P O T A T O L
```

ANNUAL FAIR
ASPARAGUS
BARLEY
BREEDING
CARROT
CATTLE
CAULIFLOWER
CELERY
CHICORY
COWS
CUCUMBER
FENNEL
FLAIL
FRUIT
HORSE
IRRIGATION
LEGUMES
MANURE SURPLUS
MEADOW
MUSHROOM
PARSNIP
POTATO
POULTRY
SCARECROW
SCYTHE
STABLE
TOMATO
TRACTOR
VEGETABLE
WEEDS

CHANGE ONE

Change one letter in each of these two words to form a common two-word phrase.

ROT BAKES

_____   _____

★★★★ The Skeleton

The object is to complete the crossword even though we've removed the black squares. You'll find the design is fully symmetrical, not only top to bottom but also side to side. To start you off we've put in some numbers that should help you flesh out the grid with black squares. The Skeleton looks difficult but once you pick out the bones, you'll soon get the hang of it!

ACROSS

1 Lessen
4 Quarrel
7 In front
10 Requiring
11 Australian marsupial
13 Tot up
14 US symbol
16 Quits (habit)
17 Weight unit
18 Throw out
20 Rotates
22 Start (of illness)
24 Authors
26 Echoes
29 Skill
30 Kip
31 More dangerous
34 Back-up (5-2)
36 Cattle farm
37 Gaped at
40 Disjoin
43 Courtroom excuse
44 Cost
45 Drug raids
46 Astern
48 Hires
49 Food energy unit
50 Sounds horn
51 Notice
52 Calls

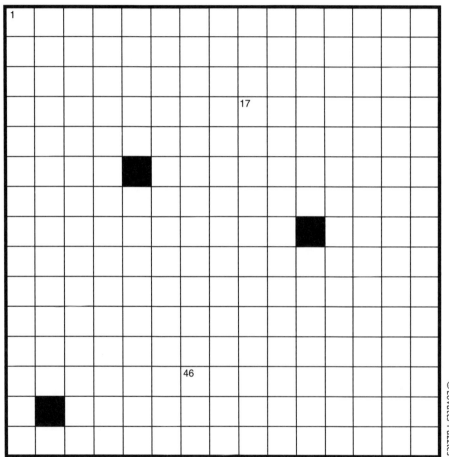

DOWN

1 Leg/foot joint
2 Not asleep
3 Pass (law)
4 Motives
5 Queer
6 Bereaved man
7 Delegate
8 Keen
9 Residue
12 Legal

15 Sharp
19 Jolting
21 Famous
22 Command
23 Ten per cent
24 Armed hostilities
25 'Tis (2'1)
27 Also
28 Snoop
32 Rested on knees
33 Steel-belted tyres

34 Regal rod
35 Sibling's daughter
37 Planet's path
38 Lariat
39 CDs, compact
40 Temptress
41 Snake poison
42 Damask blooms
47 Enemy

★ Sudoku Twin

Fill in the grid so that each row, each column and each 3 x 3 frame contains every number from 1 to 9. A sudoku twin is two connected 9 x 9 sudokus.

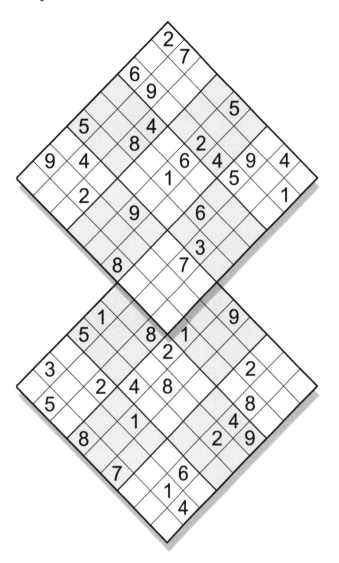

REPOSITION PREPOSITION

Unscramble LONG IDEAS and find a one-word preposition.

★★ Keep Going

Starting on a blank square of your choice, connect as many blank squares as possible with one single continuous line. You can only connect squares along vertical and horizontal lines, not along diagonal lines. You must continue the connecting line up until the next obstacle, i.e. the rim of the box, a black square or a square that has already been used. You can change direction at any obstacle you meet. Each square can only be used once. The number of blank squares that will be left unused is marked in the upper square. There is more than one solution. We only show one solution.

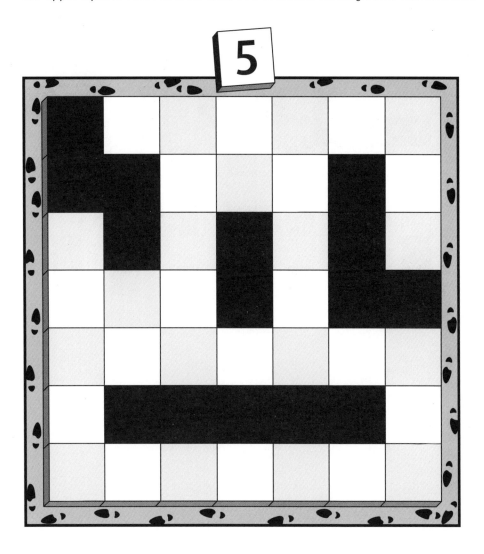

DOUBLETALK

What six-letter word means 'a supporter' or 'a unit of time'?

— — — — — —

★★★★ Teaser Toughie

ACROSS

1 It's an act
5 Gather for book
9 Expressing discontent
10 Better or best
11 Fit for a king
12 Out of the loop
13 Arouse, as wrath
15 Deck of the future
17 Parental endowments
20 Get-up-and-go
21 Spot order?
23 Deviated, nautically
27 Cardigans, usually
30 Insect larva
32 Bicker
33 Get stuck
34 Bit of regalia
35 Handout, often
36 Shifts, maybe
37 Loss, of sorts

DOWN

1 Hardly orderly
2 Vinegar acid
3 Strong suit?
4 Issue
5 Air condition?
6 Attractive item?
7 Front line, maybe

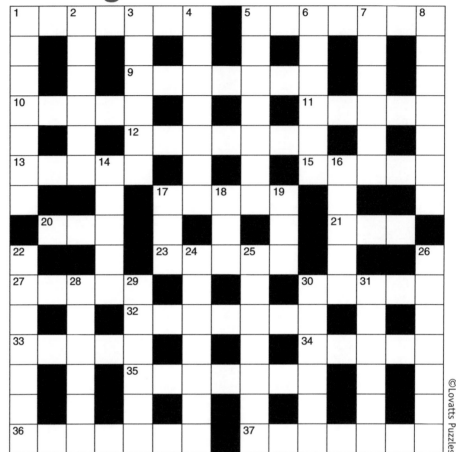

©Lovatts Puzzles

8 Connoisseurs
14 Like certain expectations
16 Examine for value
17 Steadying rope
18 Unfamiliar
19 Down
22 Lurked

24 Virtual reality folk
25 Swamps
26 Cover a point?
28 Common antiseptic
29 Balloons
30 Vex
31 Noxious vapours

★ Monkey Business

Some of the older students have been monkeying about with the BEST KIDS
BOOKS titles list in the library and have mixed up the letters of each title.
Can you unscramble each title to fix the list?

1 MOO DOG NOTHING
   By MARGARET WISE BROWN
2 HEALTHCARE VERY TINGLY PURR
   By ERIC CARLE
3 YOU TOY HAMMERER
   By P.D. EASTMAN
4 DEADWOOD APPLE TALLYHO
   By RICHARD SCARRY
5 ZERO ADO
   By ROD CAMPBELL

CHANGE ONE

Change one letter in each of these two words to form a common two-word phrase.

FIGHT FEAR

_____   _____

★ Word Pyramid

Each word in the pyramid has the letters of the word above it, plus a new letter.

T
(1) point in time
(2) insect living in organised colonies
(3) volcano in Sicily
(4) broker
(5) feeding
(6) make hot
(7) instructing

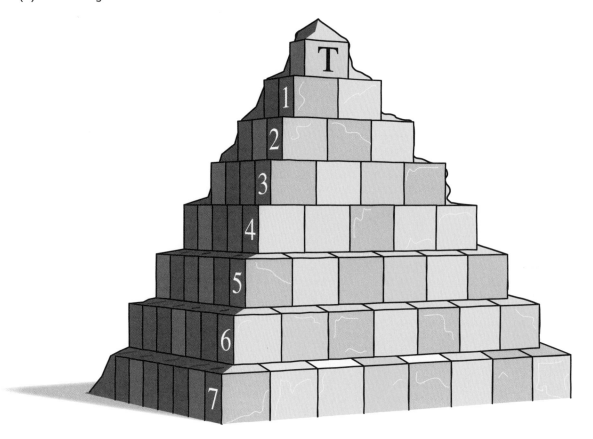

TRANSADDITION

Add one letter to I COUNTED and rearrange the rest to find a connection to learning.

★★★★ The Skeleton

The object is to complete the crossword even though we've removed the black squares. You'll find the design is fully symmetrical, not only top to bottom but also side to side. To start you off we've put in some numbers that should help you flesh out the grid with black squares. The Skeleton looks difficult but once you pick out the bones, you'll soon get the hang of it!

ACROSS

1 Plot
3 Trudges
6 Talk to God
11 Stupid
12 Louder
13 Letter writer
17 Regal
18 Long narrow crest
19 Clue
20 Road edges
22 Head monk
24 Verbally opposing
29 Anticlimax
30 Beer mug
31 Ballpoint
32 Power pole
33 Gala

DOWN

1 Couple
2 Divorce payment
4 Is short of
5 Australian wild dog
7 Ruled kingdom
8 Thread
9 Procedure to render germ-free
10 Preschools
14 Revenue-earning cargo
15 Penniless
16 Fangs
21 Cockerel
23 Wound dressing
25 Irk
26 Prelude
27 Loose fat
28 Lazy

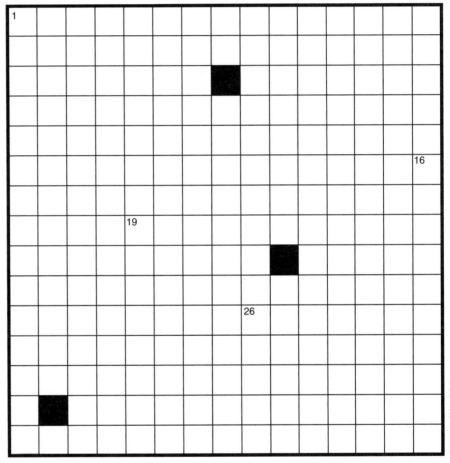

★★ Bring Me Sunshine

The arrows below point in the direction of spots where the sun will shine,
shown by the sun symbol. One spot is already shown. Can you locate
the other spots? The sun symbols cannot adjoin each other vertically,
horizontally or diagonally. A symbol cannot be placed on top of an arrow.

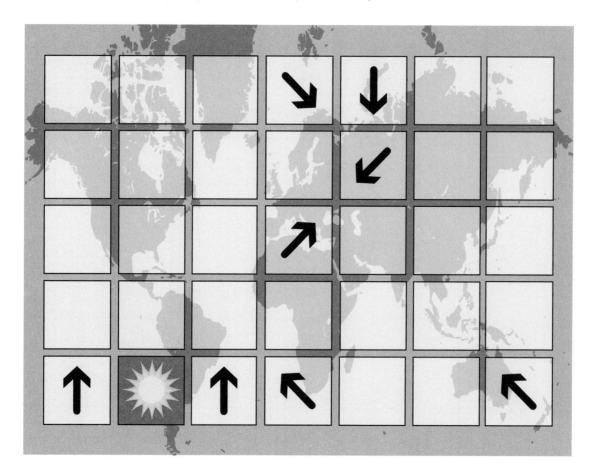

TAKE THE HINT

Use the letters from the word given in capitals to form the words that are described in
the brackets. Write your answer in the row of letter blocks. Four additional letters are
already in place.

MERCILESS (bomb)

| | | U | I | | | | | I | | S | | | |

★★★ BrainSnack®—Flag It

Each signal flag below is represented by a letter. Two signal flags strongly resemble each other per column. Which flag is the odd one out?

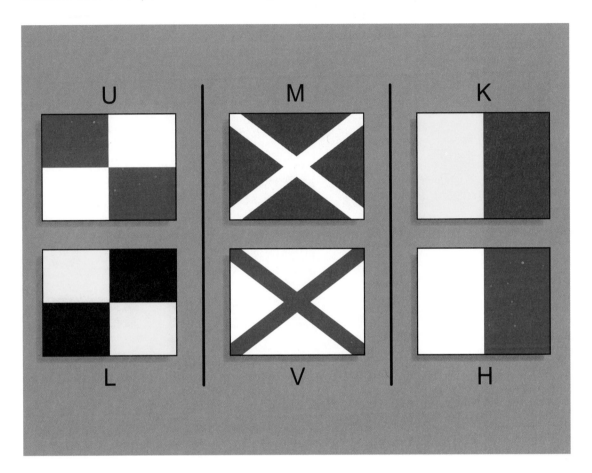

END GAME

The words you are seeking all have the letters END in them in the position indicated. When you have found all of the answers, from the clues on the right, one column will reveal the END GAME word, which might take till the cows come home.

_	_	_	_	_	_	E	N	D	To lengthen to the same extent
_	_	_	E	N	D	_	_		Disburser
_	_	_	E	N	D	_	_		A body of stories
E	N	D	_	_	_	_	_		Growth from within

★★★★ Teaser Toughie

ACROSS

1 Displaced
6 Autocrat of yore
10 Former stubble
11 Gives way
12 Personifies
14 Whale food
16 Quenching
18 Sacred Egyptian symbols
20 Tough tests
22 Vigilant
23 Far from proficient
25 In recent times
28 Entrance
29 Like tropical air
31 Life components
32 Bodily

DOWN

1 Sounds of sorrow
2 Fabled princess annoyer
3 Barrel racing venue
4 Acid artwork
5 Answers the call
7 Some Japanese cuisine
8 Uneasily
9 Like some forums
13 Cast
15 Cautioned
17 Non-intervention
19 Execrable
21 No altruist
22 Authenticate
24 Depleted
26 Standard of living?
27 Avant-garde
30 Minimal measure

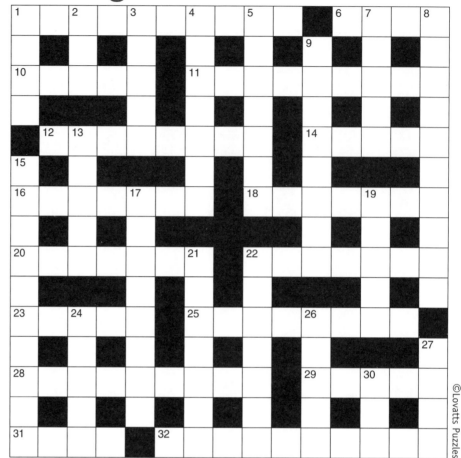

©Lovatts Puzzles

★★ The Puzzled Librarian

The new library assistant accidentally bumped into the Good Reads notice board, and the magnetic letters all fell off. The librarian remembered the authors' names, but needs some help to get the titles right, as the chief librarian will be back in ten minutes!

GOOD READS NOTICE BOARD

1. AS BAMBOO LLAMAS by WILLIAM FAULKNER
2. WAFFLES HEAL HOTLY by SAMUEL BUTLER
3. SHRINK WINS A BEWITCHED DOGGY by MAYA ANGELOU
4. WATCHMAN FROM RIDGED FORD by THOMAS HARDY
5. A THIRTEENTH CHEEK TORCH by CHARLES DICKENS
6. WELSH SARDINE by EUGENE O'NEILL
7. THIRTEENTH DESIGN by F. SCOTT FITZGERALD
8. SHAKING MEN TELL by ROBERT PENN WARREN
9. A TENTED SHAWL by T.S. ELIOT
10. DEAF MNEMONIC by JOHN STEINBECK

MISSING LETTER PROVERB

Fill in each missing letter, indicated by an X, to make a well-known proverb.

XIXHT XIXE XITH XIXE

★ Photography

All the words listed are hidden vertically, horizontally or diagonally—in both directions. The letters that remain unused form a sentence from left to right.

```
S L I D E P R O J E C T O R T
E U Q I N H C E T H M O D E L
E V M W E D A L B L E S S A H
P I E D N O M M R D P H O A T
I G G E L O E G O R A P H M Y
R N A V A T R I P O D I S A D
T E P E R E A O R I R V E R D
S T I L G F R L S R O K M O G
T T X O E T A U R E E K R N I
C I E P R T C X A L L A R A P
A N L A I O N A T U R E T P D
T G I G F L Z O O M L E N S I
N T I O T E R T H G I L A L L
O D T Y M E F A N X S W R S I
C U T S A T E L L I T E N I F
A P E R T U R E A F N E G I W
S H A R P N E S S S L I L T H
E V I T A G E N L I H M G H T
```

APERTURE
AUTOFOCUS
CAMERA
CONTACT STRIP
DARKROOM
DEVELOP
DIGITAL
ENLARGER
FILM
FIX
FLASH
HASSELBLAD
LENS
LIGHT
MEGAPIXEL
MODEL
NATURE
NEGATIVE
PANORAMA
PARALLAX
PORTRAIT
SATELLITE
SHARPNESS
SLIDE PROJECTOR
TECHNIQUE
TRIPOD
VIGNETTING
ZOOM LENS

DELETE ONE

Delete one letter from TRUE REFLECTION and rearrange the rest to find a copier.

_____

★ Cage the Animals

Draw the lines that will completely divide up the grid into smaller squares, representing cages, with exactly one animal per cage. Each cage can be as small as a single grid square. The cages cannot overlap.

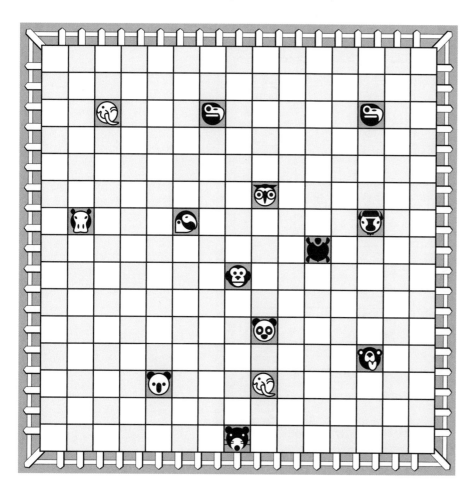

SUMMER SCHOOL

Fill the boxes with the numbers 1 to 9 to give the correct row, column and diagonal totals.

			12
3			15
			18
11	12	22	17

★★ Number Cluster

Complete the grid by forming adjoining clusters that consist of as many cubes as the number shown on the cubes. At cube 5, for example, you will have to make a cluster of five adjoining cubes. The number already shown in a cube is counted as part of the cluster. You can only place your cubes along horizontal and/or vertical lines, never diagonally.

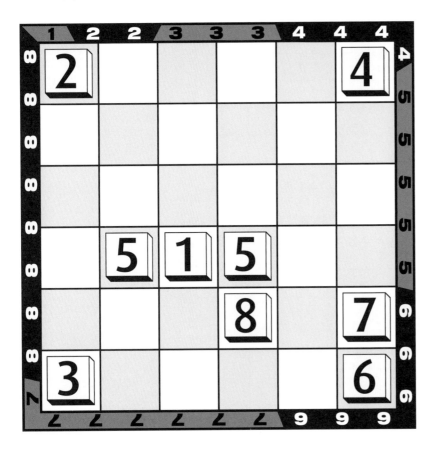

LETTER LINE

Each word below—paired with a set of numbers—is a clue to another word. This word will have the same number of letters as digits in its paired number. When you have found that word, match up each letter with its paired digit—the digit will tell you which square below in which to place the letter. When all the letters are in the correct squares, they will make a word that describes a particular type of 'mechanical device.'

1 8 5 4 6 7 2 MASTER; 6 8 1 9 5 7 MEDDLE;
4 6 7 5 8 1 RIVER; 1 3 4 5 INSPIRATION.

1	2	3	4	5	6	7	8	9	10

★ Spot the Differences

There are nine differences between these two images. Can you find them? Circle the differences on the image on the right.

DELETE ONE

Delete one letter from STUPID TALES and rearrange the rest to find triteness.

_____

★★★★ The Skeleton

The object is to complete the crossword even though we've removed the black squares. You'll find the design is fully symmetrical, not only top to bottom but also side to side. To start you off we've put in some numbers that should help you flesh out the grid with black squares. The Skeleton looks difficult but once you pick out the bones, you'll soon get the hang of it!

ACROSS

1 Sadistic
4 Church seat
6 Stared fixedly
9 Placing
10 Outskirts
11 Canines
12 Meadow
13 Boys
16 Sofas
17 Degraded
19 Candidate
22 Declare (insane)
24 Universal ages
25 Festivals
26 Copied
30 Opportunities
31 Unfriendly
32 Lustful looks
33 Failure
34 Teamed (with)

DOWN

1 Managed
2 Tense
3 Pork cut
4 Small African tribesmen
5 Prattled
6 Fine gravel
7 Jagged lines
8 Spring-cleans
14 Coffee seeds
15 Cancel (mission)
16 Wrongdoing
18 24 hours
20 Synthetic (3-4)
21 Passed (of time)
22 Collided, into
23 Suggested
24 Outdo
27 Great fear
28 Deeds
29 Snakes

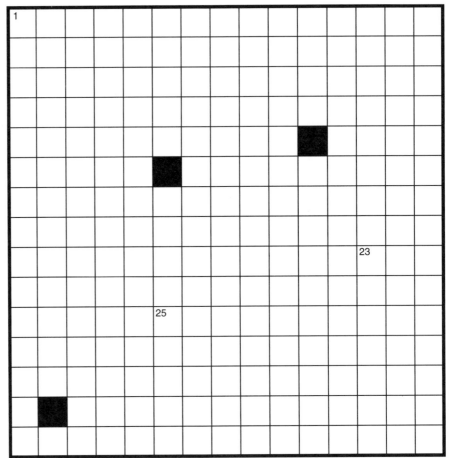

©Lovatts Puzzles

PAGE 15

For Starters

PAGE 16

Number Cluster

	1	2	2	3	3	4	4	4	
8	4	5	7	7	7	7			4
8	4	5	3	7	7	7			5
8	4	5	3	3	8	8			5
8	4	5	5	8	8	6			6
8	2	2	8	8	6	6			6
7	1	8	8	6	6	6			7
	Z	Z	Z	Z	Z	Z	9	9	9

ONE LETTER LESS OR MORE
INHALER

PAGE 17

BrainSnack®—Touchdown

1. The digits of the scores of the two teams can always be rearranged to form a consecutive series. For the last score this is 0, 2, 1.

UNCANNY TURN
TELEVISION NEWS

PAGE 18

Quick and Easy

PAGE 19

United States of America

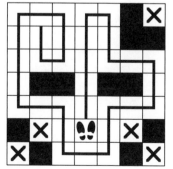

The name America is probably derived from Amerigo Vespucci, a merchant and sailor who was born in Florence.

CHANGE ONE
SWITCH ON

PAGE 20

Keep Going

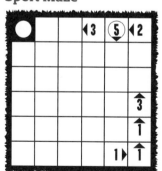

FRIENDS
Each can have the prefix ARCH- to form a new word.

PAGE 21

Quick and Easy

PAGE 22

Sudoku

5	3	1	6	4	9	2	8	7
4	6	2	5	8	7	1	9	3
9	7	8	2	1	3	5	4	6
7	8	4	3	5	6	9	2	1
2	9	6	1	7	8	4	3	5
1	5	3	9	2	4	7	6	8
8	4	9	7	3	5	6	1	2
6	2	5	8	9	1	3	7	4
3	1	7	4	6	2	8	5	9

DOODLE PUZZLE
MiddleWeight

PAGE 23

Sport Maze

ONE LETTER LESS OR MORE
CHOLERA

PAGE 24
Quick and Easy

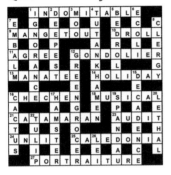

PAGE 25
Word Sudoku

E	U	G	M	I	S	A	T	Z
A	S	M	T	Z	E	G	I	U
Z	I	T	G	A	U	M	S	E
S	E	A	I	T	G	Z	U	M
I	G	U	E	M	Z	S	A	T
M	T	Z	S	U	A	E	G	I
G	M	S	U	E	I	T	Z	A
T	Z	I	A	S	M	U	E	G
U	A	E	Z	G	T	I	M	S

SANDWICH
SLEEP

PAGE 26
BrainSnack®—Crazy Cube

Solution:
Block 7.

LETTERBLOCKS
BATTERY
OPENING

PAGE 27
Quick and Easy

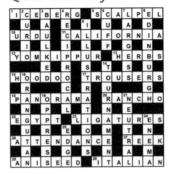

PAGE 28
Binairo

0	1	1	0	0	1	1	0	1	0	1	0
1	0	1	0	1	0	0	1	0	1	0	1
0	1	0	1	0	1	1	0	0	1	0	1
0	0	1	0	1	1	0	1	1	0	1	0
1	1	0	1	0	0	1	0	1	0	0	1
1	0	0	1	0	0	1	1	0	1	1	0
0	1	1	0	1	1	0	0	1	0	1	0
1	0	0	1	1	0	1	0	0	1	0	1
0	0	1	0	0	1	0	1	1	0	1	1
1	1	0	0	1	0	0	1	1	0	1	0
1	0	1	1	0	1	1	0	0	1	0	0
0	1	0	1	1	0	0	1	0	1	0	1

REPOSITION PREPOSITION
IN ADDITION TO

PAGE 29
Spot the Differences

DOUBLETALK
ENTRANCE

PAGE 30
Quick and Easy

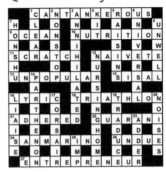

PAGE 31
Cage the Animals

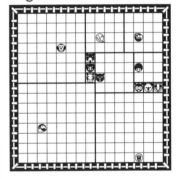

TRANSADDITION
Add S and find TELEVISION PROGRAMMING

PAGE 32
Jazz

Jazz music originated at the beginning of the twentieth century amongst dance orchestras in New Orleans.

MISSING LETTER PROVERB
Cleanliness is next to godliness.

PAGE 33

Bring Me Sunshine

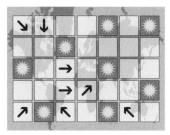

TAKE THE HINT
IRONING BOARD

PAGE 34

Quick and Easy

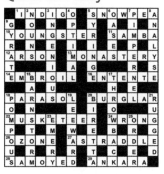

ONE LETTER LESS OR MORE
SINCERE

PAGE 35

Kakuro

7	4	8		7	8	9
	1	3		5	4	
8	7	9	5		7	4
5			8	7	6	
		6	1	2		
1	2	3		9	8	7
3	7				7	1

PAGE 36

BrainSnack®—Pedal Power

Glove 6. The left-hand gloves always have the letters ABC and the right-hand gloves have CBA.

END GAME

D I V I D E N D
E N D P O I N T
B L E N D I N G
T E N D E R L Y

PAGE 37

Quick and Easy

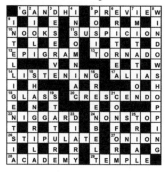

PAGE 38

Keep Going

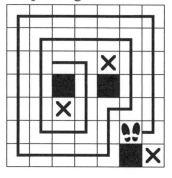

DELETE ONE
Delete S and find REBATE

PAGE 39

Sudoku

6	3	7	9	5	8	4	1	2
1	4	2	7	6	3	8	5	9
8	5	9	4	1	2	3	7	6
5	7	8	1	2	6	9	3	4
4	1	6	3	9	5	7	2	8
2	9	3	8	7	4	1	6	5
3	2	4	5	8	1	6	9	7
7	8	5	6	3	9	2	4	1
9	6	1	2	4	7	5	8	3

SUMMER SCHOOL

1	6	4	11
9	3	7	19
8	5	2	15
18	14	13	6

PAGE 40

Circuit Breaker

ache acne actin acute antic attic AUTHENTIC cane cant cent chai chain chant chat cheat chin china chine chit chute cine cite cute cutin each enact etch ethic ethnic inch intact itch nice niche nictate nucha nuchae tacet tacit tact teach tench tetanic theca thetic tunic tunicate

PAGE 41

Sport Maze

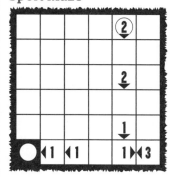

TAKE THE HINT
LOS ANGELES

PAGE 42

Word Sudoku

A	K	D	R	C	E	O	S	P
S	E	O	K	P	A	C	D	R
C	P	R	S	O	D	K	E	A
P	S	E	O	A	R	D	K	C
D	A	K	E	S	C	R	P	O
R	O	C	D	K	P	E	A	S
O	C	S	P	E	K	A	R	D
E	R	P	A	D	O	S	C	K
K	D	A	C	R	S	P	O	E

ONE LETTER LESS OR MORE
AMAZING

PAGE 43

BrainSnack®—Shirt Number

140. A red circle = 100, grey =
50, black = 10 and white = 1.
The last shirt reads 100 + 50
-10 = 140.

UNCANNY TURN
SPECIAL RECIPE

PAGE 44

Teaser

PAGE 45

Cage the Animals

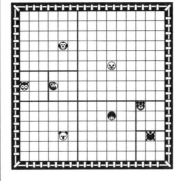

DOODLE PUZZLE
CountDown

PAGE 46

Binairo

1	0	0	1	1	0	0	1	1	0	1
1	1	0	1	0	0	1	0	1	1	0
0	1	1	0	1	1	0	1	0	1	0
1	0	1	1	0	0	1	1	0	0	1
0	1	0	1	0	1	1	0	1	1	0
0	0	1	0	1	1	0	1	1	0	1
1	1	0	1	1	0	1	0	0	1	0
0	1	1	0	0	1	1	0	1	0	1
1	0	1	0	1	1	0	1	0	1	0
1	0	0	1	0	0	1	1	0	1	1
0	1	1	0	1	1	0	0	1	0	1

CHANGE ONE
HUMBLE PIE

PAGE 47

Teaser

PAGE 48

BrainSnack®—Autumn Colours

5. There are 5 different
shapes of leaves in various
autumn colours.

LETTER LINE
INTRODUCE; REDUCTION,
INDUCE, CONDUIT, RUINED

PAGE 49

Cars

Increasingly stricter
environmental laws force car
manufacturers to look for
alternative sources of energy.

FRIENDS
Each can have the prefix
EXTRA- to form a new word.

PAGE 50

Teaser

Keep Going

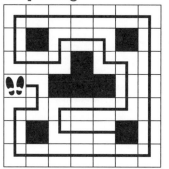

REPOSITION PREPOSITION

IN ACCORDANCE WITH

Sudoku

2	9	3	6	5	8	7	1	4
5	7	1	4	3	9	8	2	6
6	8	4	1	2	7	5	9	3
7	3	5	9	8	6	1	4	2
4	1	6	5	7	2	3	8	9
8	2	9	3	4	1	6	5	7
9	6	8	2	1	3	4	7	5
1	4	2	7	6	5	9	3	8
3	5	7	8	9	4	2	6	1

SANDWICH

SHIP

Teaser

S	A		A	U	N	T	S		R	I	D	E	R
T	A	V	E	R	N		R	I	V	E	R		U
A		I		D	I	V	A	N		G	A	G	S
C	L	A	R	E	T		C		L	I	N	N	E	T
K		T		N	E	M	E	S	I	S		A	L
E	D	I	C	T		U		S	T	A	T	U	E
D	O	O	R		E	S	C	A	P	E	D		S
	S	N	A	P		E		V		R	O	L	E
	E		N	E	E	D	L	E	D		B	A	R	D
E	S	T	E	R	S		R		T	E	N	S	E
X		I		S	P	E	C	T	R	E		T	L
C	O	N	V	O	Y		E		A	M	P	E	R	E
U		T	A	N		C	L	A	S	P		R	T
S		N	A	T	A	L		S	E	A	N	C	E
E	X	P	E	L		P	O	K	E	R		S	D

Word Sudoku

C	W	I	U	B	E	R	T	O
B	O	E	R	C	T	U	I	W
R	T	U	W	I	O	C	B	E
E	C	R	T	O	B	W	U	I
T	B	O	I	U	W	E	R	C
I	U	W	C	E	R	T	O	B
O	R	B	E	W	U	I	C	T
W	I	T	B	R	C	O	E	U
U	E	C	O	T	I	B	W	R

LETTERBLOCKS

BAGPIPE
TRUMPET

Sport Maze

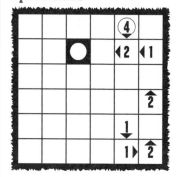

DOUBLETALK

OBJECT

Teaser

U	P	S	E	T		B	I	L	A	T	E	R	A	L
N		T		O	D	E		E		M		O		C
S		R		N	E	R	V	E		L	I	D		O
E	D	I	F	I	C	E		S	P	A	T	U	L	A
E		C		C	I	T	E		T		N		T	
N	E	T	S		B		P	R	E	C	E	D	E	
L		P	L	E	D	G	E		R	U	S	E	S	
V		R	U	L	E		S	C	A	R		N		
S	E	R	I	C		F	U	T	I	L	E		T	
P	R	O	T	E	C	T		T		S	A	S	H	
I		B		R		B	R	A	T		M		E	
D	R	O	W	N	E	D		A	D	U	L	A	T	E
E		T	E	E		Y	O	D	E	L		Z		D
R		A		E			A	L	L		E			
S	U	R	R	E	N	D	E	R		E	A	S	E	D

BrainSnack®—Star Gazer

Star 8. Stars at the same
height have the same colour.

TRANSADDITION

Add A and find NATURALIST

Sudoku Twin

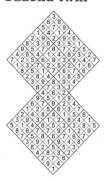

TAKE THE HINT

ACCOUNTANT

Teaser

Bring Me Sunshine

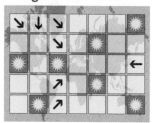

TAKE THE HINT

FOOTBALL PLAYER

PAGE 61

Word Pyramid

A, (1) Ea, (2) sea, (3) sale,
(4) lease, (5) asleep,
(6) relapse, (7) pleasure

MISSING LETTER PROVERB

All good things must come to
an end.

PAGE 62

Cage the Animals

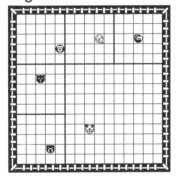

END GAME

```
I N T E N D E D
F R I E N D L Y
B E N D A B L E
U N T E N D E D
```

PAGE 63

Teaser

```
P S  REED  DIVER
DONATE NADIR   D
 O L  NEAR  LOGIC
ARCADE  BEGAN   F
S  MOGULS  TEPID
SALINA  E  EDUCE
 I I  DOSES   REP
 S SAVED LUNGS  I
TAT  SEEKS  E C
EVERT   R PARROT
DINER RECEDE   E
 A SERUM COAXED
STRUM  SILT  S X
 O MOTET EXOTIC I
ORDER  SEND  N T
```

PAGE 64

Binairo

```
I O I O I O O I I O O I
O I O I I O O I O O I I
I O O I O I I O O I I O
I O I O O I I O I I O O
O I I O I O O I I O O I
O I O I O I I O I O I O
I O I O I O I O I O O I
O I O I O I I O O I I O
O I I O I O I O I O O I
I O O I O O I O I O I I
I I O I O O I I O O I O
O O I O I I O O I I O I
```

LETTER LINE

CONFISCATE; CAFE, TONICS,
FACETS, CONCISE

PAGE 65

Keep Going

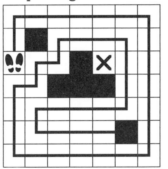

DELETE ONE

Delete one S and find
ANCIENTS

PAGE 66

Teaser

```
M P  DRAGON  MICA
AGILE  R  BALE   V
N R  TOO  EPISODE
INANE  M S  TAN  R
 A TESTAMENT  CUT
CREST   O  ALTERS
 A T  STAMMER  S
OPAL   L   E  IRIS
 I EVICTED   D N
TENDED  R   BESET
IRE  RESILIENT  E
N AIM  C  I  ATOLL
DEPRIVE  VIM  L L
E  ANON  I  EXILE
RAIN  WEDDED   D R
```

PAGE 67

BrainSnack®—Seedless

Tannin 1.40%. The sum of the
five other percentages equals
100%. Grape pulp does not
contain any tannin.

SQUIRCLES

```
B A A O C B U E
E L E P H A N T
T M R E I L R C
R O A N L L I H
A N T E L O P E
Y D E R Y T E D
```

PAGE 68

Mathematics

In most languages the word
for mathematics is derived
from the Greek word máthèma,
which means science,
knowledge or learning.

ONE LETTER LESS OR MORE

IGNORANCE

PAGE 69

Circuit Breaker

inept inert inner insert inset
instep inter intern nest news
NEWSPRINT newt nine nitre
pent pine pinner pint print
rein renin rent resin rinse
ripen risen sent serin sewn
sine sinew sinner sinter siren
snip snipe sniper snit spent
spin spine spinet spinner
sprint stein stern strewn swine
tennis tenpin tern tine tinner
trine twin twine went wine
winner winter wren

PAGE 70

Number Cluster

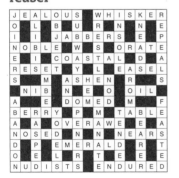

UNCANNY TURN
THE EARS

PAGE 71

BrainSnack®—Skewered

0.30. Six meatballs cost 6 x 2 = 12 sausages. 9 beef cubes cost 9 x 2 = 18 meatballs x 2 = 36 sausages. You pay a total of 16.20 for 12 + 36 + 6 = 54 sausages or 16.20/54 = 0.30 per sausage.

DOODLE PUZZLE
RedUce

PAGE 72

Teaser

| J|E|A|L|O|U|S| |W|H|I|S|K|E|R|
|O| |L| |B| |U| |R| |N| |N| |E|
|I| |I| |J|A|B|B|E|R|S| |E| |P|
|N|O|B|L|E| |W| |S| |O|R|A|T|E|
|E| |I| |C|O|A|S|T|A|L| |D| |A|
R	E	S	E	T		Y		L		E	A	S	E	L
S		M		A	S	H	E	N		R		S	
N	I	B		N		E		O		O	I	L	
A		E		D	O	M	E	D		M		F
B	E	R	R	Y		P		M		T	A	B	L	E
A		A		O	V	E	R	A	W	E		E	A
N	O	S	E	D		N		N		N	E	A	R	S
D		P		E	M	E	R	A	L	D		R	T
O		E		L		R		T		E	E	E
N	U	D	I	S	T	S		E	N	D	U	R	E	D

PAGE 73

Sport Maze

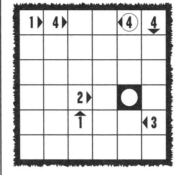

CHANGE ONE
GREEN FINGERS

PAGE 74

Word Sudoku

D	T	S	O	J	H	G	U	N
J	O	H	N	G	U	S	D	T
G	N	U	S	D	T	O	H	J
N	H	O	G	S	D	T	J	U
S	U	J	T	H	O	N	G	D
T	G	D	J	U	N	H	S	O
H	S	N	D	T	J	U	O	G
O	J	G	U	N	S	D	T	H
U	D	T	H	O	G	J	N	S

LETTERBLOCKS
BLOSSOM
COMPOST

PAGE 75

Teaser

PAGE 76

Sudoku

5	9	2	4	6	8	7	3	1
8	7	1	9	5	3	6	4	2
3	4	6	7	1	2	9	8	5
6	1	7	2	3	9	4	5	8
2	8	4	5	7	1	3	9	6
9	5	3	8	4	6	1	2	7
1	6	9	3	2	5	8	7	4
7	2	8	6	9	4	5	1	3
4	3	5	1	8	7	2	6	9

FRIENDS
Each can have the prefix DIA- to form a new word.

PAGE 77

BrainSnack®—Multiplier

65. Every multiplication is increased by a factor of 1. 13 x (4 + 1) = 65.

SANDWICH
PRINT

PAGE 78

Teaser

PAGE 79

Spot the Differences

LETTERBLOCKS
BLUNDER
BLOOPER

PAGE 80

Binairo

O	I	O	I	O	I	O	I	O	I
I	O	I	O	I	O	I	O	I	O
I	I	O	O	I	I	O	I	O	O
O	O	I	I	O	I	I	O	I	O
I	I	O	I	I	O	I	O	O	I
O	O	I	O	I	I	O	I	I	O
I	I	O	I	O	O	I	O	I	O
I	O	I	O	I	O	I	O	O	I
O	I	O	I	O	I	I	O	I	O
O	I	I	O	I	O	O	I	I	O
I	O	I	I	O	O	I	I	O	I

DOUBLETALK
SUBJECT

PAGE 81

Cage the Animals

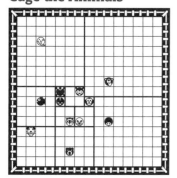

REPOSITION PREPOSITION
ON BEHALF OF

PAGE 82

Teaser

PAGE 83

Invest

When saving and investing, we put out money for a fee, thereby running a risk.

TRANSADDITION
Add A and find ANAGRAMS
NEVER LIE

PAGE 84

Bring Me Sunshine

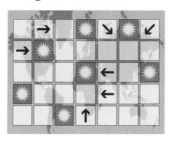

TAKE THE HINT
SLEEPING ROOM

PAGE 85

Teaser

PAGE 86

BrainSnack®—Write One

C. Starting with the middle letter M, to the right and left all letters are always 1, 2, 3 and 4 places further in the alphabet.

END GAME

M I S S P E N D
F I E N D I S H
L E N D A B L E
E N D O C Y S T

PAGE 87

Kakuro

2	9	3		9	7	2		4
7			1	6	5	9		1	5
	9	6	8		4	8	2	6
7	2	8			1	3		9
1		2	1	5		1	5	7
6	2		9	7	1		3	
	7	6			9		1	9
7	6	2	8	4		1	4	
5	8		9	1		2	7	1

MISSING LETTER PROVERB
Barking dogs seldom bite.

PAGE 88

Teaser

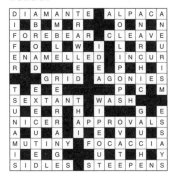

PAGE 89

Word Sudoku

T	U	W	E	R	S	B	Y	A
Y	R	S	B	A	W	E	U	T
A	B	E	T	U	Y	W	S	R
E	S	Y	A	B	R	T	W	U
U	A	T	W	S	E	Y	R	B
B	W	R	Y	T	U	S	A	E
S	E	A	U	Y	T	R	B	W
R	T	U	S	W	B	A	E	Y
W	Y	B	R	E	A	U	T	S

LETTERBLOCKS
DESPAIR
HOPEFUL

PAGE 90

Keep Going

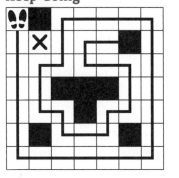

DELETE ONE
Delete A and find SOMERSAULT

PAGE 91

Teaser

PAGE 92

Sport Maze

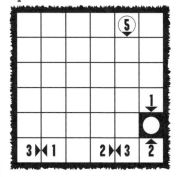

LETTER LINE
ESTABLISH; STABLE, BASIL,
SALT, SLAB

PAGE 93

Sudoku

8	2	4	3	7	5	1	6	9
3	9	1	6	4	2	7	8	5
7	6	5	9	8	1	3	4	2
1	3	2	4	5	8	9	7	6
4	7	6	2	9	3	5	1	8
5	8	9	7	1	6	4	2	3
2	5	3	1	6	4	8	9	7
6	1	7	8	3	9	2	5	4
9	4	8	5	2	7	6	3	1

SUMMER SCHOOL

2	4	8	14
3	5	6	14
9	1	7	17
14	10	21	14

PAGE 94

BrainSnack®—Kisses

L. Every name has four letters.
The difference of the location
of the letters in the alphabet
always equals 11, 7 and 3.
L - 11 = A + 7 = H - 3 = E.

ONE LETTER LESS OR MORE
RENEGADES

PAGE 95

Teaser

PAGE 96

Biology

Biology is an exact science
that studies living creatures,
forms of life and signs of life.

UNCANNY TURN
DANCING PARTNER

PAGE 97

BrainSnack®—Odd Number

9. All other numbers are composed of a number of blocks equal to the value of the number.

DOODLE PUZZLE

FatSDomino

PAGE 98

Teaser

C	H	A	L	I	C	E		C	L	A	R	I	F	Y
Y		V		R		L	O	S		N		A		A
M		A		O	R	A	C	L	E	S		T		R
B	A	T	O	N		T		L		E	L	A	N	D
A		A		I	C	I	N	E	S	S		C		A
L	Y	R	I	C		N		C		S	A	T	Y	R
S		N		A	G	A	T	E		R				M
	H	I	D		I		W		V		S	A	P	
E		I		L	U	N	G	E		O				A
V	I	T	A	L		E		G	N	A	W	S		
I		H		A	R	S	E	N	A	L		L		U
C	O	W	E	D		E		T		U	R	B	A	N
T		A		L	E	A	F	L	E	T		I		D
E		R		E		T		E		E		N		E
D	E	T	E	S	T	S		R	A	N	C	O	U	R

PAGE 99

Cage the Animals

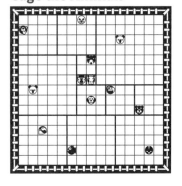

CHANGE ONE

SEA CHANGE

PAGE 100

Binairo

1	1	0	1	0	0	1	1	0	0	1	0
1	1	0	1	0	1	1	0	0	1	0	0
0	0	1	0	1	1	0	0	1	1	0	1
0	1	1	0	1	0	0	1	1	0	1	0
1	0	0	1	0	0	1	1	0	1	1	0
1	0	1	0	1	1	0	0	1	0	0	1
0	1	1	0	0	1	1	0	0	1	0	1
0	1	0	1	1	0	0	1	0	1	1	0
1	0	0	1	0	1	0	0	1	0	1	1
0	0	1	0	1	0	1	1	0	1	0	1
0	1	1	0	0	1	1	0	1	0	1	0
1	0	0	1	1	0	0	1	1	0	0	1

DOODLE PUZZLE

SevenTies

PAGE 101

Teaser

M	E	T	H	O	D	I	C	A	L		A	R	C	H
O		E		C		N		N		N	O		E	
L	O	A	T	H		S	A	N	D	P	I	P	E	R
E		R		T		U		P		E		E		
	D	E	M	E	R	A	R	A		O	G	L	E	D
I		N		L		L		S		I				I
M	I	N	D	F	U	L		S	N	I	P	P	E	T
P		U		R			T		A		A			A
O	P	I	N	I	N	G		S	T	E	R	N	E	R
S				G	O	L		O		I		Y		
S	T	A	S	H		B	L	A	T	A	N	C	Y	
I		I		T		N		D						W
B	R	O	M	E	L	I	A	D		O	K	A	P	I
L		L		N		N		E		R		M		N
E	D	I	T		E	S	T	R	A	N	G	I	N	G

PAGE 102

Keep Going

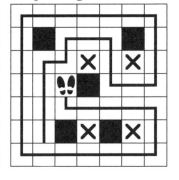

FRIENDS

Each can have the suffix -SHIP to form a new word.

PAGE 103

Word Sudoku

S	A	Z	B	L	G	E	K	Q
B	L	K	Q	E	S	A	G	Z
G	Q	E	Z	K	A	L	B	S
Z	G	B	A	Q	K	S	L	E
A	E	S	G	Z	L	K	Q	B
Q	K	L	S	B	E	G	Z	A
E	Z	G	K	A	Q	B	S	L
L	S	Q	E	G	B	Z	A	K
K	B	A	L	S	Z	Q	E	G

SANDWICH

PAPER

PAGE 104

The Gourmet

B	A	P	S		N		W	O	R	M	W	O	O	D
O		I		T	U	N	A		A		R		O	
R	O	M	A		O		C	I	N	N	A	M	O	N
S		I		C	K		H	O		E				
C	H	E	R	I	M	O	Y	A		A	L			
H		N		A			L	E	T	T	U	C	E	
	T		A	M	O	N	G		T		U			
B	R	O	W	N		U		A		A	D	A	P	T
	O		T		G	R	E	E	N		L			
C	O	R	N	I	S	H		N			T	P		
	E		P		T	E	N	D	E	R	I	S	E	
E		G	A		L		A		T		Q			
G	R	I	S	S	I	N	I		U	F	U	G	U	
G		O		T		T	U	B	E		D		I	
S	E	N	S	I	B	L	E		E		B	E	A	N

PAGE 105

Sport Maze

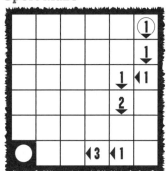

LETTERBLOCKS

AEROBIC
FITNESS

PAGE 106

Sudoku X

REPOSITION PREPOSITION
IN POINT OF

PAGE 107

Tricky Teaser

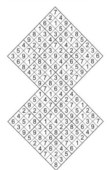

PAGE 108

BrainSnack®—Star Tripper

3124. The probe always flies to the next star system with one more yellow star.

DOUBLETALK
WIND

PAGE 109

Word Pyramid

M, (1) me, (2) emu, (3) mule, (4) plume, (5) lumper, (6) crumple, (7) plectrum

TRANSADDITION
Add S and find CANNED MUSIC

PAGE 110

Bring Me Sunshine

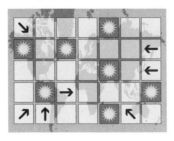

TAKE THE HINT
STEWARDESS

PAGE 111

On the Road

PAGE 112

Sudoku Twin

MISSING LETTER PROVERB
Familiarity breeds contempt.

PAGE 113

Cage the Animals

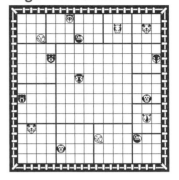

END GAME

H A C I E N D A
A D D E N D U M
R E V E R E N D
D E P E N D E D

PAGE 114

Tricky Teaser

PAGE 115

BrainSnack®—Fingerprints

Piece 2 is the only piece that fits.

DOODLE PUZZLE
One after the Other

PAGE 116

The Spy Who Came in From the Cold

13, 16, 24, 17, 19, 15, 7, 3, 29, 8, 23, 20, 14, 30, 28, 12, 21, 9, 26, 11, 5, 10, 18, 25, 22, 6 =

INV ASI ONB EGI NSA TMI DNI GHT ONT HEF IRS TMO NDA YIN JUN EAT DAW NCO DEN AME OPE RAT ION WAT ERF ALL

INVASION BEGINS AT MIDNIGHT ON THE FIRST MONDAY IN JUNE AT DAWN CODENAME OPERATION WATERFALL

LETTER LINE
REVELATION; RELATIVE, ELEVATOR, RIOT, RETAIN

PAGE 117

The Gardener

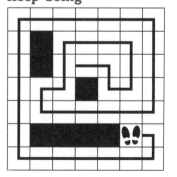

PAGE 118

Keep Going

DELETE ONE
Delete S and find COMPENSATION

PAGE 119

Athletics

Athletics is a sport that was originally closely linked to the Greek classic olympic games.

ONE LETTER LESS OR MORE
ARMCHAIRS

PAGE 120

Tricky Teaser

PAGE 121

Sport Maze

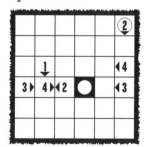

UNCANNY TURN
PUNISHMENT

PAGE 122

The Gourmet

PAGE 123

Spot the Differences

CHANGE ONE
SHOUTING MATCH

PAGE 124

Sudoku

6	3	5	4	2	8	1	9	7
4	9	7	5	6	1	8	2	3
1	8	2	7	3	9	5	6	4
5	1	4	8	9	2	3	7	6
3	2	8	6	7	4	9	1	5
9	7	6	1	5	3	2	4	8
2	5	1	3	4	7	6	8	9
7	6	9	2	8	5	4	3	1
8	4	3	9	1	6	7	5	2

MAGIC SQUARE
There are 86 ways. Apart from the 4 rows, 4 columns, and two diagonals, here are more ways that will help lead you to others: 9-14-3-8, 4-9-8-13, 15-8-9-2, 6-7-10-11, 15-14-3-2, 4-5-11-14

PAGE 125

Word Sudoku

S	A	M	X	P	N	R	O	T
N	P	R	O	A	T	X	S	M
X	T	O	S	R	M	P	N	A
M	O	N	R	X	A	T	P	S
A	S	P	M	T	O	N	R	X
R	X	T	P	N	S	A	M	O
O	N	X	A	S	P	M	T	R
T	R	S	N	M	X	O	A	P
P	M	A	T	O	R	S	X	N

DOODLE PUZZLE
MidAfterNoon

PAGE 126

BrainSnack®—Cubism

Group 2. In all the other groups two identically coloured cubes are located diagonally across from each other in the corners.

SUMMER SCHOOL

8	3	6	17
5	4	1	10
2	9	7	18
15	16	14	19

PAGE 127

Circuit Breaker

euro metro more morse mort most mote motet motte moue mouse mouser otter ours oust ouster outer outre outset rose rote roue rouse roust rout route smote some sore sort sour store storm stout stouter stretto sumo tome tore tort torte torus tote totem totter tour tout trot trout tutor utmost UTTERMOST

PAGE 128

Cage the Animals

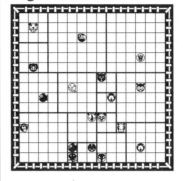

FRIENDS
Each can have the suffix -DOM to form a new word.

PAGE 129

Binairo

I	I	O	I	O	O	I	O	I	I	O
O	I	I	O	I	O	I	O	I	O	O	I
O	O	I	I	O	I	O	I	I	O	I
I	I	O	I	I	O	I	O	O	I	O
I	O	I	O	O	I	I	O	I	O	I
O	O	I	O	I	I	O	I	I	O	I
O	I	O	I	O	I	I	O	I	O
I	O	I	I	O	I	O	O	I	I	O
I	I	O	O	I	I	O	I	O	O	I
O	I	I	O	I	O	I	O	I	I	O
I	O	O	I	O	I	O	I	O	I	I

SANDWICH
NAIL

PAGE 130

Tricky Teaser

PAGE 131

Astronomy

Astronomy is one of the few sciences in which amateurs can play an active role.

LETTERBLOCKS
ENGLAND
GERMANY

PAGE 132

Keep Going

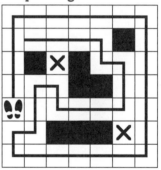

REPOSITION PREPOSITION
NOTWITHSTANDING

PAGE 133

On the Road

Sport Maze

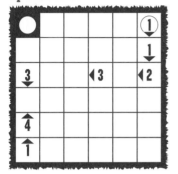

DOUBLETALK
STICK

Kakuro

6	1	7			1	5			3	2
9	2			2	9	3			4	1
5	3	7	6			8	1			3
8		8					3	5	6	
		9	4	8		6	7	4		
1	5			1	7	3			1	2
3	2	7			2	1	8			4
8		4		6			6	7	8	
4	2	9	7			1	7	8	9	

TRANSADDITION
Add S and find CREDENTIALS

Tricky Teaser

BrainSnack®—Painter

Paint 3. 6/8 of a square was coloured in with paints 1 and 4; 5/8 of a square for paint 2; and 7/8 for paint 3.

TAKE THE HINT
SPINAL CORD

Word Sudoku

R	A	B	I	T	V	L	D	E
D	E	V	L	A	R	T	B	I
I	L	T	B	E	D	R	A	V
A	V	I	R	D	L	E	T	B
B	R	E	T	I	A	D	V	L
T	D	L	V	B	E	A	I	R
E	I	D	A	R	B	V	L	T
V	B	R	D	L	T	I	E	A
L	T	A	E	V	I	B	R	D

MISSING LETTER PROVERB
Silence is golden.

BrainSnack®—Number Block

7. Every number equals the sum of the number of blocks to the right of the number and the number of blocks under the number.

END GAME
A S C E N D E R
U N B E N D E D
R E M E N D E D
A M E N D I N G

The Gourmet

Sudoku X

1	7	3	9	8	5	6	4	2
2	4	5	3	6	1	8	9	7
6	9	8	4	2	7	5	3	1
7	2	9	6	1	3	4	5	8
5	8	6	2	7	4	9	1	3
3	1	4	8	5	9	2	7	6
8	5	1	7	4	2	3	6	9
9	6	7	5	3	8	1	2	4
4	3	2	1	9	6	7	8	5

UNCANNY TURN
BAD CREDIT

Cage the Animals

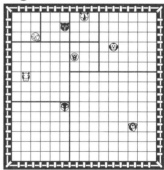

SUMMER SCHOOL

9	4	2	15
3	6	8	17
5	1	7	13
17	11	17	22

PAGE 143

On the Road

PAGE 144

Keep Going

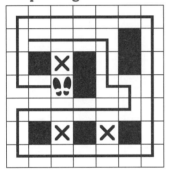

DELETE ONE

Delete S and find FANATICISM

PAGE 145

Telecommunications

In the past, if you wanted to phone someone then you pressed a button to attract the attention of the switchboard operator.

CHANGE ONE

COLD SWEAT

PAGE 146

The Gardener

PAGE 147

BrainSnack®—Energy Saver

9. The rooms located one floor higher use the average of the two rooms below.

LETTER LINE

FORMIDABLE; BAILED, LIMBO, BRIEF, BLADE, BEDLAM

PAGE 148

Monkey Business

The Lion the Witch and the Wardrobe
The Cat in the Hat
The Ugly Duckling
Charlotte's Web
The Twits

ONE LETTER LESS OR MORE

COALITION

PAGE 149

The Gourmet

PAGE 150

Sport Maze

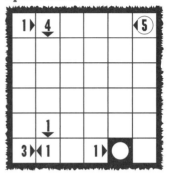

UNCANNY TURN

MUMMY

PAGE 151

Word Sudoku

P	K	Q	G	N	C	A	M	I
I	A	M	P	K	Q	G	C	N
G	N	C	I	M	A	K	Q	P
M	I	A	K	Q	N	P	G	C
C	G	K	M	A	P	N	I	Q
Q	P	N	C	I	G	M	K	A
N	Q	G	A	C	K	I	P	M
A	M	P	Q	G	I	C	N	K
K	C	I	N	P	M	Q	A	G

DOODLE PUZZLE

CoffeeBreak

PAGE 152

Spot the Differences

DELETE ONE

Delete N and find CROUPIERS

PAGE 153

The Skeleton

B	A	S	T	I	N	G		R	E	B	U	I	L	T
A		T		V	U	L	T	U	R	E		N		R
P	R	O	M	O	T	E		M	A	E	S	T	R	O
T		R		R	E		O		P		E			W
I	C	I	L	Y		F	L	U		S	E	R	V	E
S	H	E		U		U		R				N	I	L
M	U	S	I	C	A	L		S	A	D	I	S	T	S
	T			O		U		O		O			A	
E	N	D	O	W	E	D		E	S	T	E	E	M	S
S	E	A			I		N			R			I	M
C	Y	N	I	C		M	U	D		P	I	A	N	O
A		G		O		M		U		H		S		K
P	O	L	L	U	T	E		R	E	A	L	I	S	E
E		E		P	E	S	T	E	R	S		N		R
D	E	S	C	E	N	T		D	R	E	D	G	E	S

PAGE 154

Sudoku X

5	2	4	7	3	8	1	9	6
9	8	6	4	2	1	3	5	7
7	1	3	5	9	6	4	2	8
6	4	2	9	1	3	8	7	5
8	3	9	6	7	5	2	4	1
1	5	7	8	4	2	9	6	3
3	7	1	2	5	4	6	8	9
4	9	8	3	6	7	5	1	2
2	6	5	1	8	9	7	3	4

FRIENDS

Each can have the suffix -AL to form a new word

PAGE 155

Cage the Animals

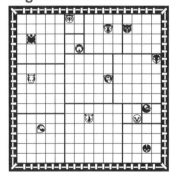

SANDWICH

HEAD

PAGE 156

Circuit Breaker

abri acid acrid arid aril aroid bail bailor baldric bardic baric bipod bipolar bird blip boil boric braid brail bridal brio broil caroli carpi clip CLIPBOARD cobia coil coir cordial crib dial diol dipolar drail drib drip idol labroid laic laid lair laird liar lido lira loci lorica olid paid pail pair parboil parodic pica picador placid placoid plaid plica podia rabi rabic rabid radio raid rail rapid rial ribald roil

PAGE 157

BrainSnack®—Parking Space

Car 11. All white and red cars are parked nose inward. All blue cars are parked with the nose outward except car 11.

LETTERBLOCKS

SPIDER
CRICKET

PAGE 158

Agriculture

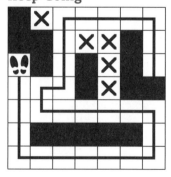

Agriculture produces food as well as other goods such as flowers, fur, leather and biofuel.

CHANGE ONE

HOT CAKES

PAGE 159

The Skeleton

A	B	A	T	E		R	O	W		A	H	E	A	D
N		W		N	E	E	D	I	N	G		A		R
K	O	A	L	A		A	D	D		E	A	G	L	E
L		K	I	C	K	S		O	U	N	C	E		G
E	J	E	C	T		O		W		T	U	R	N	S
A		I		O	N	S	E	T		T		O		
W	R	I	T	E	R	S		R	E	P	E	A	T	S
A	R	T		D			D		N			N	A	P
R	I	S	K	I	E	R		S	T	A	N	D	B	Y
N		N		N		R	A	N	C	H		I		L
O	G	L	E	D		D		E		S	E	V	E	R
R		A	L	I	B	I		P	R	I	C	E		O
B	U	S	T	S		A	F	T		R	E	N	T	S
I		S		C	A	L	O	R	I	E		O		E
T	O	O	T	S		S	E	E		N	A	M	E	S

PAGE 160

Sudoku Twin

REPOSITION PREPOSITION

ALONGSIDE

PAGE 161

Keep Going

DOUBLETALK

SECOND

PAGE 162

Teaser Toughie

PAGE 163

Monkey Business

Goodnight Moon
The Very Hungry Caterpillar
Are You My Mother?
What Do People Do All Day?
Dear Zoo

CHANGE ONE

LIGHT YEAR

PAGE 164

Word Pyramid

T, (1) at, (2) ant, (3) Etna,
(4) agent, (5) eating,
(6) heating, (7) teaching

TRANSADDITION

Add A and find EDUCATION

PAGE 165

The Skeleton

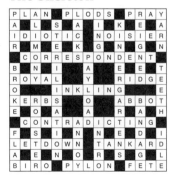

PAGE 166

Bring Me Sunshine

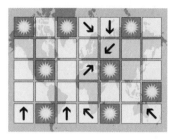

TAKE THE HINT

CRUISE MISSILE

PAGE 167

BrainSnack®—Flag It

Flag M. Every pair includes a
red and white flag. The other
flag in the pair has the same
pattern but all the colours are
different. Only one colour is
different on flag M.

END GAME

C O E X T E N D
E X P E N D E R
L E G E N D R Y
E N D O G E N Y

PAGE 168

Teaser Toughie

PAGE 169

The Puzzled Librarian

1) *Absalom, Absalom!*
2) *The Way of All Flesh*
3) *I Know Why the Caged Bird
   Sings*
4) *Far From the Madding
   Crowd*
5) *The Cricket on the Hearth*
6) *Ah, Wilderness!*
7) *Tender Is the Night*
8) *All the King's Men*
9) *The Waste Land*
10) *Of Mice and Men*

MISSING LETTER PROVERB

Fight fire with fire.

PAGE 170

Photography

The word photography is
derived from Greek; it literally
means writing with light.

DELETE ONE

Delete L and find
COUNTERFEITER

PAGE 171

Cage the Animals

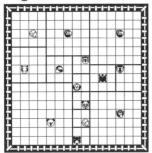

SUMMER SCHOOL

2	1	9	12
3	7	5	15
6	4	8	18
11	12	22	17

PAGE 172

Number Cluster

2	2	4	4	4	4
8	8	7	7	7	7
8	5	5	5	6	7
8	5	1	5	6	7
8	8	8	8	6	7
3	3	3	6	6	6

LETTER LINE

MOUSETRAPS; MAESTRO, TAMPER, STREAM, MUSE

PAGE 173

Spot the Differences

DELETE ONE

Delete one S and find
PLATITUDES

PAGE 174

The Skeleton

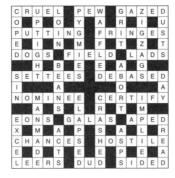

C	R	U	E	L		P	E	W		G	A	Z	E	D
O		P		O		Y		A		R		I		U
P	U	T	T	I	N	G		F	R	I	N	G	E	S
E		I		N		M		F		T		Z		T
D	O	G	S		F	I	E	L	D		L	A	D	S
		H		B		E		E		A		G		
S	E	T	T	E	E	S		D	E	B	A	S	E	D
I				A				O				O		A
N	O	M	I	N	E	E		C	E	R	T	I	F	Y
		A		S		L		R		T		M		
E	O	N	S		G	A	L	A	S		A	P	E	D
X		M		A		P		S		A		L		R
C	H	A	N	C	E	S		H	O	S	T	I	L	E
E		D		T		E		E		P		E		A
L	E	E	R	S		D	U	D		S	I	D	E	D